Radical
Theology

Radical *Theology*

SELECTED ESSAYS

Don Cupitt

POLEBRIDGE PRESS

Cover and interior design by Robaire Ream
Cover illustration by Robaire Ream

Library of Congress Cataloging-in-Publication Data

Cupitt, Don.
  [Selections. 2006]
  Radical theology : selected essays / Don Cupitt.
    p. cm.
  Includes bibliographical references and index.
  ISBN-13: 978-0-944344-97-2 (pbk. : alk. paper)
  1. Theology, Doctrinal--History--20th century. 2. Philosophical theol-
ogy. 3. Religion--Philosophy. I. Title.

  BT28.C85 2006
  210--dc22

                            2006022110

In Memory of
John A. T. Robinson
1919–1983

CONTENTS

ACKNOWLEDGEMENT

I thank the Cambridge University Press for permission to reprint no. 10 in this volume, "One Jesus, Many Christs", which first appeared in S. W. Sykes and J. P. Clayton (eds.), *Christ, Faith and History: Cambridge Studies in Christology,* first published by them in 1972. The SCM Press of London has kindly allowed me to reprint essay no. 15, 'John Robinson and the Language of Faith in God' from Colin Slee (ed.), *Honest to God: Early Years On*, 2003.

INTRODUCTION

After twenty-five years or so of being—or at least, of being described as—'a radical theologian', I'm beginning to wonder what the phrase means. It keeps some questionable company, and I have to start by dissociating myself from many of the ideas and the hopes that have kept it alive for the past forty years. Happily, there is also a positive side, for the very idea of 'radical theology' is uniquely Christian and says something very important about where religious thought stands today, and what it must go through.

Radical theology is not very old: I think the expression first came into common use during the 1960s, in connection with the much-publicized work of Thomas J. J. Altizer and William Hamilton in the USA, and John A. T. Robinson in England. Before that date, the phrase 'radical theology' is very scarce. The first use in the 1790s of the phrase 'radical reformation' was political, not religious. In Britain, a radical reformer was a person who was sympathetic to the principles of the French Revolution. To ordinary reformers it is important, in a time of profound upheaval, that one should be able to maintain the continuity of the great institutions. Radicals, on the other hand, are people who are happy to emphasize *dis*continuity. To a political radical around the years 1790–1819 it seemed obvious that the established British constitution—'Church and King', and the 'Three Estates of the Realm'—was irrational and unjust. Radicals sought thoroughgoing, root-and-branch reform, and were entirely ready to be labelled unorthodox and subversive. The most prominent group of them were the associates of Jeremy Bentham and James Mill, the 'Philosophical Radicals'. The philosopher Alan Ryan comments:

> Philosophical Radicalism has always struck historians as an un-English phe-
> nomenon, in that it was an ideologically coherent political movement which
> paid as much attention to the intellectual foundations of its programme
> as to the mechanics of getting its supporters into power. Neither Bentham
> nor James Mill . . . could tolerate such commonplaces as 'it's all very well in
> theory', with their implication that something other than theory ought to
> guide our practice. . . . As James Mill put it, 'What is theory? The *whole* of the
> knowledge, which we possess on any subject, put into that order and form in
> which it is most easy to draw from it good practical rules. . . . To recommend
> the separation of practice from theory, is, therefore, simply to recommend
> bad practice.'[1]

If we now switch all these considerations from the political field into the religious, we understand how it is that the radical theologian dreams of writing a work of theology that is at the same time a revolutionary manifesto. He dreams of spelling out exactly what is wrong with the Church's faith and institutions, and how they need to be reformed; and spelling it all

1

out with such simple cogency and clarity that the case once stated will be irresistible. In short, he tries to write the sort of book that will make everyone see sense and will change the world.

It's a taxi-driver's dream. It is well known that there are certain topics on which every taxi-driver knows all the answers. One of them is what should be done about the tax system, and another is how to solve the problem of traffic congestion on the roads. A further problem of much the same profundity is the question of what the higher clergy should do in order to get the people back into church. Every day the Archbishop of Canterbury gets a sackful of letters from people who are determined to tell him *exactly* how to do his job. He employs a group of people who draft standard replies and send them out, because he knows he's never going to get a letter that really *does* contain the Right Answer, just as nobody is ever *really* going to write the book that gets it all right, and speedily changes everything.

Can we cite any historical examples of a book that changed everything, and that quickly prevailed because it made such a clear and compelling case? Perhaps the best example that can be quoted is *The Origin of Species*; but even that book is very far from having yet won universal acceptance of its argument, and it will be many more years yet before even those of us who most love and admire it will be able to claim that we have fully assimilated all its implications. In philosophy, ethics, religion and politics, where everything is disputed, it is even less likely now that anyone will ever write a major text that speedily wins universal assent. Without labouring the point, may I perhaps name the four most highly-publicized works of 'radical theology' published in Britain before J. A. T. Robinson's *Honest to God?* They are Thomas Arnold's *Principles of Church Reform* (1833), the symposium *Essays and Reviews* (1860), J. Y. Campbell's *The New Theology* (1907), and E. W. Barnes' *The Rise of Christianity* (1947); and, dear reader, you will not be insulted if I suggest that you have barely heard of any of them. They are all feeble, dated works, deservedly forgotten.

—Which is why radical theology has a bad name. Radical theology tempts people to hope they can make a very big splash with only a very small talent. Radical theology rests on the old and basically *theological* belief in a ready-made objective Truth out there, a Truth that when it is revealed will shine forth like the sun, all-conquering and indisputable. But alas, in the most important matters—the great questions of philosophy, ethics, religion and politics—there is no readymade, unarguable Truth sitting out there waiting for the hour when it is due to be revealed. The most that a rational person can set out to do is to join the ongoing public debate, and by questioning some assumptions and contributing some new arguments try to change the tone of the conversation, and influence the evolving consensus of public opinion.

Of course it is true that we live amidst an acute crisis of faith. Most of traditional Christian belief is no longer tenable: we just don't have sufficient reason to think it true. Everybody knows by now that the classical arguments for God's existence do not stand up, that traditional ideas about the authority of the Bible have broken down, and that most of classical Christian doctrine, from the Fall of Man to the Blessed Trinity, is simply *not* 'scriptural', in the sense usually claimed. Even in its own day and on its own terms, much of it was mistaken, or at least ill-made. Today, there is an increasingly wide gap between the world-view that is inculcated by church services and the world-view that we all operate with in everyday life. *But we all know this already!* We've known it for many generations, and merely pointing it out in a very loud voice will not change anything at all. It will not persuade church leaders to budge one inch. And in any case, what can *they* do? They have far less power than people suppose. They think they are doing pretty well if they merely succeed in keeping the peace within the church.

All of which may well lead us to wonder why there is radical theology at all. What can it realistically aim to do, and how far can it hope ever to achieve its aims? One can understand that it is very often written as an expression of disappointment and frustration.[2] Why does the decline of religion continue so remorselessly, and why is everyone so fatalistic about it? Why are those few of us who do try to do something to purge, reform, and renew religion regarded as villains for our pains? Two hundred years of critical theology have demonstrated beyond reasonable doubt that all our religious belief-systems and institutions are human, with a human history. *We* created every bit of them, including all those ideas about revelation, about Holy Tradition and about dogmatic immutability. We created it all, so why can't *we* reform and renew it all?

The radical theologian may have honest and intelligible motives, but as I have been suggesting many temptations lie in his or her path. There's the temptation to try to make a big splash with rather modest abilities. There's the temptation to suppose that it will be sufficient merely to replace a false and outmoded belief-system with a shiny new, up-to-date and suitably abridged belief-system. And there's the temptation to suppose that people will be interested in, and will want to *act upon*, what one has to say. They won't—because the Church is not and perhaps never was chiefly for people who have a deep and serious intellectual interest in religion. On the contrary, the Church is for people who want to keep up comfortable old habits and associations, who want a feeling of reassurance and self-righteousness, and are happy to live by a ready-made Truth. They are content to go on slumbering peacefully. They want to be *delivered from* the extreme terrors and joys of real religious thought, and nothing is so effective a protection against religious terrors as conforming church membership. At least ninety-five percent of the hierarchy and of church members alike will never see the radical theologian as a liberator and rebuilder: instead, they will *always* see him as a troublemaker, a nuisance, an irritant who should be got rid of.

Finally, the radical theologian is still caught up in the old 'theological' illusion that there could be, there is, one truth for everybody, a sacred and universally-authoritative ideology that means the same to everyone, everywhere. But of course in our postmodernity ideology is dead, and the old religious vocabulary of symbols and doctrines is broken up and scattered across the whole of culture. It has become incurably fragmented, ubiquitous and polysemic.[3]

One begins to understand why, despite its seemingly honest and laudable intentions, radical theology since about the time of D. F. Strauss has not been able to achieve anything very much. It has often caused an ephemeral sensation, but it has not succeeded in making a lasting difference to the way people think about religion.

Nevertheless—and as I have been saying—there is also a positive side. There remain reasons why I persist with theology and am not ashamed of the label 'radical theologian'. Radical theology is faith *in extremis*. It is written by people who have experienced the breakdown of popular, orthodox dogmatic faith, and have been compelled to discover the scarce and very extreme terrors and joys of real religious thought. The radical theologian is a person—oddly enough, usually male so far[4]—who has passed through a moment of violent discontinuity, and has struggled to remake or rediscover faith on the far side of the loss of faith. Because he has gone through something like death and resurrection he believes that he is still within Christianity, even though he has entirely lost the popular sort of faith. Christianity, it seems, includes also its own moment of self-cancellation: faith's day includes its own midnight. Why?—because, paradoxically, the very considerations that caused the loss of faith then go on to recreate faith in a new and more powerful form. The decline of popular (orthodox, traditional) faith since the Enlightenment has been caused by the spreading realization that we and we alone made it all: we humans have ourselves slowly evolved our own language, our own worldview, our own religions and moralities, and the whole of our own knowledge. None of it was supernaturally communicated to us from above: we made it all up. That simple proposition is now so blindingly obvious that one wonders how any human being can pretend to believe otherwise whilst looking another in the eye. So thoroughgoing 'religious naturalism' is unavoidable, and popular faith collapses. We are on our own. There is no other way to religious truth except by working it out for ourselves by studying philosophy, by experimenting with one's own life, by debating with others and so on. Gradually one begins to recover: gradually one learns that convictions which one has struggled for and acquired oneself, the hard way, and then has gradually crystallized in debate with others, are far stronger and more valuable to us than any amount of traditional ready-made truth. All orthodoxies fail: truth is always 'heretical', because only religion that you have *yourself* made up and fought for can in the end avail to help you.

On my view then, radical theology is a personal struggle for a new and better kind of religion on the far side of the loss of the older sort of popular, traditional, ecclesiastical faith. It is, inevitably, highly autobiographical. One writes progress-reports. You may say that my own progress, such as it is, has been slow and hard-won, with much flailing and floundering; and I can't disagree with you. But in a matter as great as this any progress at all, however slight, is wonderful and something to be very grateful for.

Radical theology has flourished (if it can be said to have 'flourished'), at historical turning-points and times of break-up—for example, in connection with the beginnings of popular revolt towards the end of the Middle Ages, on the left wing of the Protestant Reformation, in response to the Enlightenment and the French Revolution, after the First World War, and most recently since the final breakdown of traditional European culture and the rise of a new media-led and post-traditional Pop culture in the early 1960s. If radical theology flourishes today, it is perhaps chiefly in response to the realization that the old ecclesiastical sort of Christianity is now in galloping decline and in a few generations will be effectively extinct. Unless we can quickly make up something to replace it, the outlook for humanity is very bleak.

So far I have been describing radical theology as a distinctively Christian enterprise, an attempt in an age of terminal decline to take Christianity through its own death and rebirth. Of all the great religious traditions, the Christian is the one best prepared to attempt a move of this kind. It is the only religion that tries to foresee its own self-transcendence. It sets up a symbol, and then knocks it down: it dies, and then finds a new life on the far side of its own death: it doesn't exist for its own sake, but looks forward to disappearing into its own fulfilment: it is the absolute religion in the sense of being always able entirely to relativize itself, and thereby to surpass itself.

This highly dialectical character of Christianity makes it peculiarly liable to value-reversals. Within the Christian tradition it is easy to point to examples, both of extreme pessimism and world-denial, and of extreme optimism and world-affirmation; and also to examples both of endorsement of the state and civil society, and of thoroughgoing rejection of and flight from them.

To take world-pessimism first, the bulk of early and medieval Christian thought considered that in this life we are so continuously threatened by the ups and downs of fortune, by time and chance, by corruption and death, that no secure and lasting happiness is possible here below. If you really seek blessedness, you must become a monk or nun and invest all your hopes in the next life. But since the later Middle Ages there has been a very large-scale turn to this world. The average person's life, at least in the advanced countries, has become very much longer, healthier and more predictable, and most people surely think that a happy life here below for nearly everyone ought in principle to be attainable. There is no reason why we should not now take up a much friendlier attitude to time, contingency, sense-experience and the body. In fact, we almost identify blessedness with the love of life, and that means this life which we are now living.

Religious attitudes to civil society have undergone similar reversals, more than once. Early Christianity took the view that human nature is so rebellious and disorderly that for as long as history lasts there will be a continuing need for strong government. Even in a highly advanced country like the USA, the skin of civilization is thin. When there is a power-cut on a dark evening, people very quickly start breaking windows and looting shops. It has happened, *recently*. People must be governed, and if necessary they must be ruled *by force*, because even tyranny is better than anarchy—something that the early Christians knew so well that they prayed for the state even when it was persecuting them.

Right up to Luther and beyond, the main body of Christianity continued to take a pessimistic view of human nature and to see the state as a necessary dyke against sin, with the right and the duty to impose strict discipline upon the population. The only escape that you could hope for was to argue that if the Christian machinery of redemption were ever to succeed in overcoming human rebelliousness and transforming human nature, we might be able to create a free and redeemed society in which people could safely live together in peace, without the constant threat of force to keep them in order. This more optimistic attitude towards the possibility of a peaceful and free society grew steadily stronger during the Enlightenment, as people gradually began to believe that a law-abiding orderly system can evolve from below and be self-maintaining, both in nature, and in culture. Order doesn't *have* to be thought of as always needing to be imposed from Above. At the same time, during the Enlightenment, it also began to be thought that general respect for the Law and for social conventions is in everyone's interest, and therefore can be maintained just by education and by the general consent. The ultimate sanction of force can be kept in the background: it does not *have* to be so prominent as it was in the past.

On this basis a good deal of modern naturalistic explanation developed. People began to see life, and language, and culture, and values as all of them having evolved from below. Everything is a human improvisation, and none the worse for that. And on the same basis modern liberal democracy developed: government from below, government that is given its authority by the governed, and that keeps its authority by being careful to maintain the consent of the governed. The leading liberal democratic country for over two centuries has been the USA, and it is well known that Americans are so convinced that democracy is the best form of government for everyone that they are inclined to think that it is the *natural* form of government—the form of government under which people feel most free, and the form of government that people everywhere would welcome, if given a chance. Yet there is something very paradoxical about this, for liberal democracy rests upon unusually optimistic assumptions about human nature. It is assumed that people are naturally rational enough to see the advantages of, to choose, and to stick to a peaceful, cooperative, and law-abiding form of life, that is agreed by all and is best for all. But are people everywhere *really* so very sober and sensible as that? It seems not; and in any case optimism about human nature co-exists in the American tradition with the classic Christian doctrine of the Fall and Original Sin.

From this discussion I now want to draw a few conclusions. First, Christian attitudes to Nature, to human nature, and to the State have varied greatly, from the traditional right-wing pessimism that aims to keep wickedness in check by imposing strict discipline everywhere, to the most starry-eyed liberal optimism. Virtually every view that can be held, has been held, and the variety has been such that it seems unlikely that we will ever settle permanently upon just one agreed set of valuations of Nature, of human nature, and of the State. What happens is rather that the pendulum swings, and the whole complex of attitudes and values shifts, from one period to another, according to the mood and the needs of the time.

But, secondly, it doesn't follow that religious thought merely follows and reflects current cultural fashions. On the contrary, religious thinking always includes a political dimension, and makes an implicit comment on current political values. I think I should explain why and how this is so.

In recent years I have come more and more to see human beings as creatures of *feeling*. When we acquired language and became reflective, we humans became able to reflect on how we feel about the human situation as a whole: how we feel about 'Life', or 'Everything', or 'It All', as we say. This sort of cosmic feeling expresses our attempt to grasp what we are, what there is around us, how we fit into It All[5] and, in general, how we stand. Or, to try another pregnant phrase, **How It is with us**. So for me religion is cosmic feeling, seeking a satisfactory vocabulary in which it can express itself and come to a satisfactory understanding of and valuation of our human condition.

The feelings I have about this most general of all topics vary greatly. In my most optimistic and affirmative moods I want to express cosmic joy, satisfaction and gratitude for life. But in my very darkest moods I feel that the human condition is tragic and that 'the nature of things' or It All is indifferent or even sometimes actively contemptuous of us humans, casually ruining us with no redress or consolation of any kind whatever. Those are the two extremes, approximately represented by the young Wordsworth and by King Lear. Life is such that at different times either of them, or any intermediate valuation of the human condition, may seem to be rational. There is hardly any limit to the variety of languages in which we may wish to describe the human situation, and hardly any limit to the variety of feelings we may have about it, so extraordinarily ambivalent is it. And I have already suggested that we may take an almost equally wide range of views about the basic benignity or the basic malevolence of civil society, and of individual human nature.

How then do we ever manage to settle upon any general working picture of things, to live by? I suggest that we follow the method of art. Like a film director or a novelist who produces a personal vision of life, we select and highlight or even caricature in order to produce a distinctive vision of the human scene which suggests an appropriate attitude to life, and an appropriate set of values to live by. In short, I am suggesting that a religion is a specialized kind of life-map that provides us with its own distinctive set of metaphors, stories and values to live by. Of these stories, the most important will of course be the great narrative of Fall and Redemption that sets out to show us what is presently wrong with us, tells us how we can each of us play our part in the process of putting everything right, and promises us that we will in the end see the final perfect state of everything. All of which helps to explain the mixed and rather ambivalent character of our life-experience now—and also brings us very close to politics. For it is of course a fact that *all* political ideologies in the West, this past 250 years or so, have borrowed extensively from Christian doctrine. Politics as we know it is semi-secularized religion, for it offers us a diagnosis of what is wrong with our world, it offers us membership of a community that is actively working to put things right, and it offers us some kind of vision of an attainable Good Society to work towards. Politics cannot of course promise everything, and even Marxism did not promise to conquer the basic metaphysical limits of human life, Time, Finitude and Chance. Even in the fully communist society people will still be finite, liable to accidents and ultimately mortal. But so far as our human life-world is concerned, religious and political diagnoses and prescriptions are moving in much the same territory. The only difference between them is that religion is concerned, not only with intrahuman relations in the human world, but also with the greater question of how we humans are to relate ourselves to the larger non-human backcloth—It All, or Everything—against which we act out our lives. Religion is bigger than politics, for it asks a wider and more difficult question about how we can be happy about It All. Like how we are to cope with all the things that politics cannot pretend ever to be able to deal with, such as Time, Chance and Death.

I am suggesting, then, that religion is bigger than politics, because in addition to dealing with the questions of justice in the human world that politics also deals with, it—that is, religion—also tackles the much bigger and harder questions of how we are to describe and to come to terms with the basic metaphysical limits of our life. For about the last two centuries these have been seen as our one-way movement through time towards death, our constant vulnerability to chance and to our biological limitations, and our finite, imperfect knowledge and powers. No amount of scientific progress, no amount of political progress is ever likely to emancipate us entirely from these constraints. We need to find ways of seeing them clearly, and of saying Yes to life in the face of them—and that is what religion helps us to do. And because religion is right to say that the greatest problems of life are *more* than political, religion has the right to criticise the kind of arrogant totalitarian politics that tries to make a god of the State and to make political ideology into compulsory dogma.

My conclusion, then, is that an adventurous radical theology that is attempting to renew religion today will naturally be found criticising the laziness and decadence of our current religion and politics, and trying to clarify the scope and the limits of the political by renewing our ability to see and to cope with the great *trans*-political issues of life. We'll get politics right when we understand its limits. There are issues that are much, much bigger than national sovereignty, bigger than 'the economy', and bigger even than social justice. And when we see that clearly, we'll get things in perspective.

* * * *

The whole body of my writing, over about four decades now, has been an attempt at radical theology. I have been trying to discover and spell out something that might serve us today as true religion. But my writings have been both voluminous and (understandably) very unpopular, with the result that my ideas are not well understood even in England, my own country. In this present book I have collected some eighteen shorter pieces, written between 1972 and the present day, that have so far either not been published or have appeared only in rather out-of-the-way places. They begin with this Introduction itself, which was first written for the 16th Annual Conference of the Sea of Faith, held at Leicester, England in July 2003.

Next, Part One contains five pieces about radical theology and the darkest hour of faith. No. 1, 'Religion without Supernaturalism' opened the first-ever Sea of Faith Conference, held at Loughborough, Leicestershire,

England in 1988. We were so apprehensive in those days that no list of those attending was circulated, and photography was banned! No. 2, 'Radical Apologetics' was my contribution to the second Sea of Faith Conference in 1989. No. 3, 'Traditionalism versus Radicalism' was one of two pieces written for a multi-faith symposium about radical theology in each of the major religious traditions. Unfortunately the symposium never appeared, mainly because it turned out that no other great religion *has* a tradition of radical theology in the sense in which Christianity has—probably because no other faith has such a strong sense of the course of its own historical development.

No. 4, 'After Liberalism' was written for *The Weight of Glory* (1991), a *Festschrift* for a dear and lamented friend, Peter Baelz. Finally, No. 5, 'Learning to Live without "Identity" ' (1997) was written for another symposium that never appeared, but was to have been titled *The Future of Jewish-Christian Dialogue.*

Part Two changes tack. It simply contains four sermons, all of them first addressed to student audiences, which show how I set about preaching radical theology, and in particular the controversial 'non-realist' doctrine of God. In 1980 I published *Taking Leave of God* (London: SCM Press), and became instantly notorious. John Robinson was at that time Dean of Chapel at Trinity College, and was very pleased by the sudden resurgence of radical theology after a decade of relative silence. He asked me to preach at Trinity College, and 'God Within' was written for that occasion. It was later published in a 'sermon-festschrift' for Robert Runcie: Dan Cohn-Sherbok (ed.), *Tradition and Unity* (London: Bellew Publishing, 1991).

In 1982 I followed up with *The World to Come.* At that time I was still getting some church invitations, and was asked to introduce the book at Great St Mary's, the Cambridge University church, and then to debate it with John Robinson before a student audience. No. 7 below, 'Make Believe', is my opening statement: it was first published in Robinson's own final collection, *Where Three Ways Meet* (London: SCM Press, 1987).

No. 8, 'Religious Experience' is an ordinary Emmanuel College sermon of about 1986, which was first printed in Dan Cohn-Sherbok (ed.), *Glimpses of God* (London: Duckworth, 1994). No. 9, 'God Beyond Objectivity', another Emmanuel sermon of about 1991 is included here because it plays with and looks forward to the more radical ideas of my latest thinking. It appeared in Dan Cohn-Sherbok (ed.), *Using the Bible Today* (London: Bellew Publishing, 1991).

These four sermons are almost the only ones that survive from my most active years as a pastor. I include them to show how one radical theologian has set about what others call 'teaching the Faith'. In today's church, sermons are nearly always remarkably undemanding, but there seems to be no reason why preachers should not aim higher. Certainly I had no trouble attracting an audience.

Part Three contains a group of academic essays about Jesus Christ and humanism. From the outset I have been highly aware of the contrast between 'the Jesus of History' and 'the Christ of Faith'. The historical Jesus was a Jewish man, a moral teacher, an ironist and someone firmly locked into one very particular historical context. How can he at the same time be an ideal and iconic figure, the universal divine Cosmocrator? In various ways, this theme is explored in No. 10, which was first published in S. W. Sykes (ed.), *Christ, Faith and History* (Cambridge University Press, 1972), and in No. 11, *The Finality of Christ*, which appeared in an Appendix to the first edition of my *The Leap of Reason* (London: SPCK/The Sheldon Press, 1976). It was also the theme of my contribution to the symposium, John Hick (ed.), *The Myth of God Incarnate* (London: SCM Press, 1977), here reprinted as No. 12.

No. 13, 'Religious Humanism' was written as my opening statement in a debate with the well-known secular humanist Nicholas Walter, staged at the fourth Conference of Sea of Faith (UK), in 1991. It alludes to a rather Hegelian theme to which I have often returned: we shouldn't be afraid of humanism or regard it as an enemy, because Christianity is above all the religion that is always turning into humanism, as the divine comes back into the human realm and is disseminated through it. And anyway, as we come to appreciate the extent to which everything is historical and everything is mediated by (human) language, so a form of radical humanism becomes inevitable. We have no access to any non-human point of view, and (more radically) there *is* no non-human point of view. Only for *us* is the world *world*.

Finally, Part Four contains two recent pieces. 'An Apologia for my Thinking' was written for advance circulation to people attending a day conference about me organized in 2002 by David Hart, then of the Multi-Faith Centre at Derby University. It was first published in the *Emmanuel College Magazine 2001–2002*.

No. 15, on 'John Robinson and the Language of Faith in God' was written for a 'study day' at Southwark Cathedral, marking the occurrence in March 2003 of the fortieth anniversary of the first publication of *Honest to God*. As usual, people were making patronising remarks about John Robinson, and I retorted that he has been much misunderstood. Like the German theologians whom he quoted, Robinson was aware—as very few of the British *were* aware at that time—that we live after Nietzsche and after the Death of God. Robinson was not trying to undermine the faith: he was rebuilding it.

The summaries (No. 16) are examples of my many attempts to make my ideas more intelligible to popular audiences. Unfortunately, I couldn't find a good enough one about ethics. Finally, the little 'Envoi' raises the question of success and failure, on my mind as I reach the age of 70. I think I'll stick with a comment about this that I made in the 1980s. I knew before I came out as a radical that my efforts would not be popular. One cannot realistically hope for 'success', but one can at least stick it out and try to leave a body of work big and varied enough to cause the Church lasting irritation. To that I'll add in the light of more recent experience that although it is by definition 'heretical', creative religious thinking can be the source of extraordinarily intense happiness. I'd even say that creative religious thinking just *is* true religion. That is why I maintain that the religious society of the future will not have any creed: instead, it will supply an environment in which people are emboldened to develop out of themselves their own religious outlook—rather as a writer or a painter labours to find her own voice. For you the real 'radical theology' is your own voice, if you can but find it: hence the determined creedlessness of Sea of Faith and its encouragement of active participation by all members.

Emmanuel College   Don Cupitt
Cambridge, UK

Part One

Radical Theology and the Midnight of Faith

1

RELIGION WITHOUT
SUPERNATURALISM (1988)

Since this Conference (*the first Sea of Faith Conference*) was announced I have learnt of the existence of associations of Radical Baptists and Radical Methodists, both of them societies which do valuable work in their respective denominations. I've just heard, too, that there's a group of radical Jews. But this meeting remains probably the first national gathering of radical Christians that is fully open and undenominational. After the publication of *Honest to God* in 1963, John Robinson held a number of 'Hooks and Eyes' conferences at Bletchingley in Surrey, but the theological debate at that time now looks to have been liberal rather than radical in temper, and those who attended the Bletchingley gatherings might perhaps today be more at home with the Modern Churchpeople's Union than with us. I rather doubt if they would have understood the phrase in our conference details, 'completely non-supernaturalist', in anywhere near as plain and strong a sense as some of us do. Graham Shaw and I have both declared in print for straightforward religious naturalism; that is to say, the view that you can be, and should be, a religious person, whilst fully acknowledging that religion is wholly a human historical product in every part of it. Yet we remain practising Christian priests. We would, I think, both of us say that the intellectual and spiritual crisis of the times is now not less but more severe than it was in the relatively innocent early 1960s. A whole further generation of rapid change has made all the problems not less but more acute, while at the same time it is harder now than it was then to get an honest public debate about them going.

However, we do not yet know what spectrum of views there may be to be found among us, nor how much common ground there will be. Our discussions during the next two days should help to answer that question. Meanwhile, I am going to try to mark out the field, by suggesting that there are a few points on which we are probably agreed at the outset, and also saying something of the background against which we meet.

The points on which I guess we may agree are five: First, we all believe that religions matters a great deal to society. Society needs a common faith. At the very least, this will surely consist of a stock of shared universal symbols, themes and values, a vocabulary in which it is possible to pursue and debate publicly the great questions of life, and recognised rituals to mark public occasions.

Secondly, we would not be here unless religion mattered to us individually. We are the sort of people who need to work out where they stand. We may end up deciding that we are in exile from religion, or we may end up deciding that we are undecided; but at any rate we are not indifferent. The subject matters to us, and it matters a great deal.

Thirdly, we are people for whom the religion that matters most is that of the Jewish-Christian tradition. Nobody starts from scratch. Everybody has a native language. Everybody is already in a particular cultural, moral and religious tradition. We must use the vocabulary we've inherited. If we should wish to say something new about religion, it will stand the best chance of making sense if we couch it in the form of a reinterpretation of the Judeo-Christian religious tradition which is our background.

Fourthly, whether we actually call ourselves Christians or not, we do already find ourselves committed to many things that are distinctively Christian. I will mention two in particular. The first is the religious human-ism that finds perhaps both its first and its greatest expression in the art of Rembrandt. Rembrandt's subjects are always comically plain, plump and ordinary Dutch people, old and young, female and male, Jews as well as gen-tiles. But whether he is painting a biblical subject or not, Rembrandt more than any other artist consistently imbues the most ordinary human beings with intense religious pathos and dignity. Florentine painting had sought to make the human form holy by investing it with ideal Greek beauty. To that extent, Italian humanism is doubtless half-pagan. But Rembrandt's human-ism is Biblical. In Rembrandt's vision divine love and compassion are so strong that he makes a holy thing out of the human body in its ugliness, suffering, weakness, old age and death. That is Judaeo-Christian religious humanism, and it is the peculiar glory of our tradition. Translated into humanitarian ethics a century or so later, it has transformed much of the world in the past two centuries. We are probably all of us Christians in the broad sense that we owe allegiance to those values, and would be ready to join with others in rituals that affirm them.

There is also, I guess, a second sense in which we are all of us already Christian. We want to align ourselves with the Church in those many countries where it is the only effective focus of opposition to a cruel and despotic government. The modern State is primarily concerned with money and power, control and security, economic management and defence. The administrative techniques now available to the State in this electronic and media age are immensely strong, and it easily becomes totalitarian. In many countries the ordinary person has no other defence except his or her membership of a great and enduring society expressly concerned with the affirmation and maintenance of moral and spiritual values. That society is the Church. It is needed as a stronghold, a rallying-point, a focus of dissent and a guardian of values in an increasingly barbarous world. I think I would say more than that: it's not only totalitarian politics, but while there is an alternative value scale in conflict with the dominant value scale you have possibilities of freedom which are not present in any society in which the culture has been totalized or systematised. The conflict between Church and State, between two different orders of values, in Christian society is uniquely creative.

So far I have suggested that we are, I hope, in agreement—or we may be: it is for you to say. I have suggested that we are agreed in thinking religion important both to society and to the individual, and in thinking that any religion we can succeed in working out for ourselves is likely to take the form of a reinterpretation of Christianity. At the very least, we need to preserve a certain vision of the religious worth of common humanity. Although its sources go back to the Bible, this Christian religious humanism has come to fruition only in modern times. Its first peak was in seventeenth-century Holland. It subsequently peaked again in nineteenth-century humanitarianism and in twentieth-century human rights movements. It is our only great modern religious achievement. It is Christian, and it must at all costs be preserved because it is just about the only thing we have left to make our life worth living. And the proper instrument for defending human values and human rights is the Church.

So there is plenty for the Church to be and to do—which brings me to the fifth and last of our points of agreement. We are in varying degrees exasperated that the Church insists on handicapping herself by remaining needlessly locked into a world-view that is well over 300 years out of date. Why should we have to be time-travellers in order to go to church? That wasn't true until the seventeenth century. Why has it had to become true since the seventeenth century? The problem is that Christian worship, theology and institutions are still locked into a very ancient, once universal, type of religious ideology. According to this the whole visible world, but in particular our own society, is related to an invisible spirit-world as downstairs is to upstairs in a great house. We are the servants, they up there are the masters. Everything comes down from them. They define reality, they decide everything, they allocate to us our roles, our duties and our fates, and they have all power and authority. They know everything and their influence is ubiquitous, but unseen. Gods are very strange beings. They seem to hover on the margins of consciousness, as if we feel them to be something like guiding and accusing thoughts in our own minds, while at the same time we are acutely aware of their boundless power to control events in the external world. We daren't displease them, and various professional groups, such as priests and prophets, are called upon to mediate between them and us.

This system of thought used to prevail all around the world in thousands of locally different forms. It always comes down to people from their past as well as from above, so that there is a kind of Triple Alliance: the gods above, the leading figures in society and the Fathers from the past all join hands to confirm each other's authority over us. It looks as if the ancient religious ideologies had the function of conserving cultural values, defining ethnic identity and maintaining social control. The message was: to survive, stick to these figures, stick to these values, stick to these practices, stick together. The whole scheme was about authority: the authority of the past, the authority of society, and the authority of the gods above. There is always intense concern to get the whole system communicated intact to the next generation, so that the teaching of religion to the young remains a politically sensitive topic to this day.

For most of its history Christianity lived in the slave society of antiquity and the feudal society of the Middle Ages. Naturally, it has come down to us packaged in a religious ideology of the kind I've described, but with a very special emphasis upon rank-order and degrees of authority, power and control both in Heaven and on Earth. Developed classical Christianity, as it existed from the fourth to the seventeenth centuries, had as a result three main features. First, it was very strongly supernaturalist. The Christian's worship and aspiration were wholly oriented towards the heavenly world above. Secondly, the entire cosmos was made out of ascending chains of unequal relationships. In church we celebrate inequality non-stop. To that extent, classical Christianity was surprisingly anti-humanist—at any rate by the standards of a modern Christian. Thirdly, because the hierarchy control theology as they control everything else in the Church, theology is designed to serve their interests.

In the late seventeenth century the whole system rather suddenly broke down in Europe, as vast changes in science, in historical knowledge, in politics, in morality and simply in consciousness got under way. The last great documents from this country (i.e. England) of the old order were *The Book of Common Prayer* (1662) and *Paradise Lost* (1667). At once, modern critical and liberal theology began trying to break Christianity out of the old supernaturalism, the old feudal cosmology and the old clerical control. But the first generation—the generation of liberals like John Locke, the Deists and so on—failed to modernise the Church, and all subsequent generations have also failed. (The best hope may have been the 30 or 40 years after the French Revolution.) Because of this failure the Church has been in slow decline for three centuries. The good news is that the waning of her old social power has made possible the emergence within Christianity of our modern religions humanism; the bad news is that the Church's doctrine, worship and vocabulary remain unreformed.

By now the difficulties are of such long standing that we scarcely notice any longer how very queer the situation is. Ethically of course the Church has to live in the modern world and cope with the political, economic and technical facts of modern life. So the Church in many ways has had to mod-ernise herself in ethics: she simply couldn't function if she didn't. But her beliefs, her language and her worship are in sharp conflict with her ethics. They belong to something like a childhood world that passed away three centuries back. The whole faith has dropped into the past tense. How could we have let it happen? The Church has perversely ghettoized herself, and condemned herself to marginality.

The fact that so much of Church doctrine is simply not tenable any more lays a heavy and unnecessary burden upon people of good will. They have become Christianity's unhappy lovers, fellow-travellers, or reluctant exiles. If we question them, I think we find they most often mention three stumbling blocks: theological realism, dogmatic theology and ecclesiastical power. On the question of theological realism, we hear from them some-thing like this: 'The Church undoubtedly still takes a realistic view of God as an all-powerful personal Spirit on whom the world depends for its existence from moment to moment, and who is out there whether we believe in him or not.' 'Now', people tell us, 'I see the value of belief in God as a vehicle for cultural ideals, as supplying a transcendent perspective upon our lives and as at least notionally unifying all our experience. But I cannot quite take a fully realistic view of God, so I cannot belong to the Church.' On the ques-tion of dogmatic theology, people say to us something like this: 'The Church undoubtedly regards her dogmatic faith as a body of saving, supernatural truths revealed to her by God. Now I see the point of Christian dogmatic beliefs, when they are at work in the Liturgy and so forth, as efficacious signs of moral change and personal spiritual growth—as when, for example, one dies and rises with Christ, and understands the language as (so to say) helping through the imagination to facilitate moral change in oneself. But such an understanding of the sense in which the Church's faith is true falls so far short of the Church's own that I don't think I can function in good faith as a fully paid-up member of the Church.' And on the question of ecclesiastical power, the fellow-travellers tell us: 'The Church is a mighty historical institution, a hierarchy of spirtitualised masculine power that is always, inevitably, coercive, repressive and allied with the haves. But Jesus was one of the poor, an outcast, a heretic and a loser. The contradiction is so overwhelming that unless the Church turns herself upside-down and actu-ally becomes the poor and the heretics, it is more honest to keep away.'

At least since the time of Hegel, liberal theology has been addressing itself to just these objections. We have been saying to the honest fellow-travellers: 'Nowadays the Church is no longer so rigidly supernaturalist and authoritarian as she was in the past. You don't have to be a theological realist. You *can* take a symbolist view of dogma. And the modern Church has become humanitarian and sincerely cares for freedom of thought and human rights and the poor. So we truly think a person like you doesn't have to live in self-imposed exile. You can honestly belong to the Church.'

This would sound good if the Church were consistently willing to back it, but notoriously she isn't. The Church is still completely controlled by the clerical Establishment. Their personal authority and power depend upon objective and God-guaranteed credentials. So they have to take a realist or objectivist view of Christian language. They've got to have their visible proofs of their own authority. So they believe in things like the Petrine Commission, the Apostolic Succession, the Real Presence and so forth. But liberal theology has always argued for inward, spiritual, symbolic and ethical interpretations, which have the side-effect of weakening clerical power. So the liberal theologian has got to be repudiated.

A well-known historical example of this is the doctrine of the Eucharistic presence. There is always a direct correlation between the degree of realism about Christ's presence in the bread and wine and the extravagance of the claims made for the spiritual power and authority of the priest who consecrates them. Rome teaches transubstantiation and a high doctrine of the priesthood, whereas at the opposite extreme Ulrich Zwingli's non-realist view of the presence of Christ's body and blood—he speaks of the bread and wine as mere symbols (*nuda signa*)—is at once understood by people of the 'catholic' persuasion as being anti-sacerdotal, and therefore wrong. Such is the extent to which theology functions as clerical ideology.

So liberal theology fails because it must always get shipwrecked on the Rock which is Peter, that is, the interests of the professional clerical Establishment. For the clerics, truth is always 'high'. And you must also know their special sense of the word 'high': a high doctrine is a doctrine that magnifies the cosmic importance of the clergy, the sacraments, redemption, the Church or whatever. There are always overtones of cosmic feudalism, and supernatural backing for priestly authority. Religious truth thus gets hijacked. And because over these past three centuries Peter, the clerical Establishment, has therefore inevitably rejected liberal theology, theology has shrunk: it has vanished from the culture at large and has become a purely internal affair of the Church—that is, of the clergy. At the Lambeth Conference the Bishops can take it for granted that they are the Church, and theology is about them. As for thinking laypeople, most of them voted with their feet long ago.

Today the argument has moved on. Liberal theology belongs to the nineteenth century. It is too late to attempt to arrange a new concordat between our present culture and an appropriately revised Christianity. Matters have gone too far for that. A cultural holocaust is under way in which the whole of our psychic past, philosophical, religious and ethical, is perishing. We are finding that traditional concepts and idioms are breaking up and becoming unintelligible to us year by year. Only a few years ago we still thought we could understand them, but now they are disintegrating. The words are becoming hollow even as we use them. Nihilism is becoming rampant.

The great variety of the comments and questions that have been proposed already by members of the Conference is perhaps an indication of the turmoil of our times. No doubt your questions will be pursued in the discussion groups. But let us not suppose that there are somewhere, somehow, experts with ready-made answers. To think that would merely be to reinstate the old dogmatism. The true position is somewhat different. Religious naturalism is the doctrine that religion is a product of history. It is we human beings who together over the centuries have developed the languages, the cultures and the various 'houses' of meaning and value within which peoples live. Religion is obviously a part of this process and indeed central to it. Like art, religion has mysterious depths even though, also like art, it's just man-made. We are visionary animals, artists and mythmakers who can live only in and through imaginary worlds. There *are* only imaginary worlds. Our various worlds of faith are like great communal works of art that we slowly evolve. It was we who built them to live in: now we must rebuild them.

Those theologians in the nineteenth century who first, following Schleiermacher, described the Christian task as the building of the kingdom of God on earth had already glimpsed what I am now trying to say. They were declaring in veiled language that we make truth, we build the Church, we are the creators. There are no ready-made answers. We ourselves must become our own answers. We've got to re-design Christianity. We must make new religious truths. The work is ours.

2

RADICAL APOLOGETICS (1989)

In the Conference (i.e. Sea of Faith II, 1989) programme I was billed to speak about 'Radicals and the Church', no doubt with my most recent book in mind. But I have had second thoughts: it has struck me that we radical and liberal Christians probably spend too much time looking at the Church, complaining about its reluctance to change, arguing for drastic revision or reduction of its doctrinal claims, defending the legitimacy of our own position and so on. I fear we may give the impression that we exist mainly as a protest movement parasitic upon the main body of Christianity, without anything very interesting to say on our own account. That impression is confirmed by much secular comment on radical theology. Many of our ablest contemporaries think that the old Augustinian Christianity, whether true or not, at least made very great and important claims and was worth arguing about, whereas modern liberal and radical theologies are so diminished and so vapid that it is not worth spending time on them. Our secular friends commonly see us merely as symptoms, casualties of the decay of Christendom. We have got a very long way to go before we can persuade them that a new and reformed Christianity is actually in sight, and is going to be important to them.

That is why I now want to suggest that we should end this conference by turning our thoughts away from our relation to the Church and the past and towards the question of what we have to say to our most thoughtful contemporaries. The problem we face is this: if we agree with and accept their characterization of the modern world, why do we believe that religion is needed at all, and why our particular sort of religion?

The philosophy I have in mind tends to be called linguistic philosophy or anti-realism in Britain, post-structuralism or semiotics in France, and pragmatism or constructivism in America. This is heavy jargon, but the leading ideas are very simple. Whereas our human life used to be grounded in a timeless metaphysical world, we now live simply immersed in an ungrounded, historically-changing flux of human communication and practice. Truth is temporary, truth is what works, truth is the state of the debate. Meaning is usage, a word simply is the ways it is currently being traded. There are no objective Truths or unchanging Meanings. Everything is human, relative, dialectical and a matter of interpretation.

This strange new world of ours was brought into being by the combination of Romanticism, industrialism and mass-communications. Its typical art-forms are the novel and the feature film. Its prophets appeared nearly two centuries ago. The first philosopher to picture all of reality as one immanent process of dialectical development was Hegel. But like other, later, historicist thinkers Hegel maintained that there was a sort of necessity in the way the world unfolded. The march of Spirit was a regular advance towards a final perfection of universal freedom, consciousness and reconciliation. This claim that there were still laws, guaranteeing progressive advance towards an ultimate Goal of the whole process, made Hegel's innovations more acceptable by making it appear that he was fulfilling and completing the tradition, rather than repudiating it in favour of a fresh start.

Hegel can also, however, be seen as a radical. He was saying that metaphysics is over. That is, the kind of philosophy that predominated from Plato to Kant Is finished. Our new awareness of the historicality of human life and the cultural programming of every human mind means that it is no longer possible to ground our knowledge and our moral values directly in the eternal order, as if history and culture did not exist. We see now that our knowledge-systems and moralities are period pieces, historically-produced and not just absolute. Beliefs and moralities are in future going to have to be explained 'horizontally', in terms of their historical development, socio-cultural context and function and so forth. Although the implications of this were not fully spelled out until Nietzsche, Hegel already introduces us to a world in which everything, everything, is shifting, horizontal, interconnected, human, a game with constantly moving goalposts, a world without any enduring and objective meanings, values or truths.

Is this nihilism looming up and making us shiver, or is it merely normality, the way things are nowadays and nothing to be alarmed about? Richard Rorty, in *Contingency, Irony and Solidarity* (Cambridge, 1989), evidently thinks that words like nihilism are overheated, for he prefers the cooler term 'irony'. He explains the word irony by saying that each of us has a 'final vocabulary' to which we resort when debating the great questions of life and when trying to articulate our most cherished beliefs, values and moral commitments. An ironist is a person who—perhaps through living in a multicultural society and through having a strong sense of historical change—has radical and incurable doubts about her own final vocabulary. She's ironical because she has a dual attitude to her own deepest convictions. It is as if for her these things are certainties about which she is chronically uncertain, absolutes that she knows are only relative, truths which she knows are only true-for-her-and-not-for-others. She says, 'There are many other vocabularies, and some of them seem to work as well as mine. I don't see any truly independent criteria by which to judge that mine is the best one, or the truth. Anyway, I have found that my own final vocabulary develops as my life goes by. My beliefs and I are fluid, changing things. I don't have either a fixed position or a fixed identity. I am an ironist in that I am both firmly committed to my own final vocabulary, for in it I define my very self, and yet at the same time also uncommitted, because it and I are always open to revision and change.'

Rorty clearly thinks that in an advanced liberal society which is plural and changing we should regard irony thus defined neither as a plight nor as a spiritual crisis, but simply as a perfectly manageable and usual condition. We should give up nostalgia for the old days when preachers and philosophers reckoned they could tell us the One Truth and give us authoritative guidance. In advanced liberal societies the job of the moralist and spiritual guide is taken over by film directors, novelists and such like. These artists communicate in a rather indirect way through fictions, dramas and art. They don't pressurize us so much as their forerunners did. They tell stories, open up new angles on life, disseminate new metaphors and new descriptions, and by these means help us in the continuous work of re-appraising and modifying our own final vocabularies.

As for putting into effect the new life-possibilities that art may open up, that is the job, says Rorty, of utopian politics. In advanced liberal societies the work once done by religious symbolism and the practice of religion is done instead by art and political campaigning.

Rorty, then, wants us to accept all this, to accept universal contingency and continual change and rethinking, without nostalgia and without any recurrence of the old impulse to deify something or other. Critical thinking means that you have no absolutes. Rorty is particularly insistent that we should not deify language—an interesting warning against what he clearly thinks is a serious temptation just now.

I agree with Rorty that we (that is, many people, of whom he is one, I am another and you perhaps are a third) now find ourselves having to live without old-style metaphysical or theological underpinning for our final vocabulary. I agree: for me too everything is contingent, a product of history and open to reassessment, including all my own ideas about God and metaphysics. There are no guarantees and no certainties. Nothing is entrenched and everything is negotiable. Like Rorty, I don't want even to try to go back to a time when there were 'absolutes'. I differ from Rorty only in that I find that to survive, in our postmodern universe made only of contingencies, relativities and interpretations, I need more spiritual resources than Rorty's rather uncomplicatedly optimistic account supplies. We are confronting a world in which everything that is most dear to us may disappear at any time. Like us, all our values and standards are rootless, fleeting and insubstantial. My beliefs and values have a history behind them, I can fairly claim that they work and make sense for me now, and I can give them my wholehearted allegiance. But I can't make myself, or them, or anything immortal. And this realization of universal transience is the Buddhist Void or Nothingness. It demands something like a Buddhist spirituality, and like an artist's selfless devotion to work, if we are to survive. Wholly to be given to the utterly-fleeting calls for a very special mixture of attachment-and-nonattachment, an intense but utterly non-possessive love that it takes a religious discipline to produce.

The job of religion now, I'm suggesting, is to give us the selflessness and the poise to survive in the modern world, and to be creative and productive people. Without religion, I believe we are threatened by pessimism, nihilism—and fundamentalism.

We can I believe already imagine a reading of the Christian Gospels along such lines. Consider the Sermon on the Mount, for example, as teaching that eternal life is to be completely and self-lessly absorbed in the present fleeting moment. Creative love and creative work are a kind of ecstasy in which we can forget ourselves and escape the fear of clock-time. Or consider how we might reinterpret Jesus' death for us. Dying, he passed into the Void for our sakes. He saw the Nihil as he died (Mark 15.34), and his having gone into it then helps me to go into it now. We are all going to have to put our heads into the black sock, you, me, everybody. He had to. Dying with Christ in the practice of religion, we go into the Nihil with him. We experience it while we are still alive. We die before death, and we are thereby liberated for eternal, non-egoistic life now. If I have already died to death in this way I can accept my own insubstantiality and that of everything else, and live free from anxiety. That is religion. It is the triad, life-death-eternal life. It is a daily practice of death-and-rebirth through which we are continually born anew and made able to live creatively.

Richard Rorty does not want us to deify anything, he says, but like a number of other twentieth-century philosophers, critics and theorists, he tends I believe to oversesteem the imaginative writer. For him as for so many postmoderns religion has turned into writing; that is, imaginative writing has become a substitute for religion as a source of inspiration. Here again I disagree. It was a misfortune that after the Reformation the new presbyter often turned out to be just as domineering as old priest had formerly been, and it will be equally a misfortune today if the preacher is similarly replaced by the writer. We'll be stuck with yet another clericalism, this time the clericalism of writers and entertainers. Long ago Moses said, 'Would that all the Lord's people were prophets!'—and quite right, too. We don't want a world in which writers and entertainers do the creating for us. In the advanced media society everyone is a star or a fan, all products have to be attractively and fashionably packaged and life is dominated by designers, trend-setters and box-office values. Too much bad art makes for a profoundly alienating type of society, and to deliver us from it we need a religion, and not just writers. In any case, the record of writers as moral guides is no better than that of earlier clerical castes. So, we would prefer to see a world in which everyone is morally free, creative and productive in her own life. We are talking about a religious discipline oriented not (as so often in the past) towards loyal and devout acceptance of authority, but towards the conquest of nihilism, the affirmation of life, its investment with significance and value, and the production of innovation.

So we don't need art to replace religion, but we do need a renewed, creative religion to replace the religion we have. It will require a rich symbolic vocabulary, developed from the one we have inherited, in which people can test themselves out in debate with one another.

A final and parenthetical comment: although it is preoccupied with the question of creation and creativity, radical theology is not concerned with the high-level theories in physical cosmology which some people still consider to be of religious interest. The reason is that Big Bang theory, or standard-model cosmology, has nothing at all to do with religion. Physics belongs to the margins of life and language, and physical theory has as such no more religious authority or interest than any other sort of technical or scientific theorizing. The questions of nihilism, the conquest of nihilism and the doctrine of creation, in philosophy and religion, are concerned with how ordinary people in their daily lives can together make sense, make good and make their world. That is a sufficiently-important question to be going on with, and it is already sufficiently abyssal for even the stoutest heart.

Try this, for example: if the world's all interpretations, how can one even say as much? Is it true that there's no truth? And if we have talked our way into nihilism and are trying to talk our way out of it, how can we demand a rigorously austere and even nihilistic kind of religion—in the name of Truth? Worst of all for us clumsy Westerners, how can you seek inner emptiness, clarity and integrity in a region so thick with reflexive paradoxes and ironies?

3

TRADITIONALISM VERSUS RADICALISM (1997)

Around the world the great religions have three features in common: they are traditional, they are patriarchally-governed, and they have traceable historical origins—or, at least, all of them point with pride to certain great creative figures whose work helped to originate or to enrich their own tradition. But the religions may be unaware of the potential for conflict here. If Tradition contains timeless truths, how come that it had an historical beginning? How did some people seemingly create it, and how did other people get to be its monopoly franchisees?

Tradition is everywhere proclaimed to be a plenum, holy and immutable. It cannot be altered in even the smallest detail. It supplies a complete and final ideology for a whole people to live by: cosmology, salvation-history, rules of life, and procedures for communicating with the supernatural world. A whole pyramid of father-figures are supernaturally-accredited to act as Holy Tradition's professional guardians, interpreters and ministers. They are the makers of religious Law and the rulers of the religious society.

Yet this great edifice all had a beginning; and the creative people in whom Tradition began cannot themselves have been traditionalists. Furthermore, only after the authority of Tradition has become established can there develop a priestly ruling class who claim to derive their own power and authority from it.

So a contradiction arises: Tradition is holy, complete, perfect and immutable—but it did arise, and it has a history. Within the holy community nobody is allowed ever to have any radically new ideas—but the community could never have come into historical existence unless some venerated figures long ago had dared to think new thoughts. Is it not strange that the pure religious creativity, for which we worship the founder, can never, ever, be shared by his followers?

Thoroughgoing traditionalism, in the technical sense, was a nineteenth-century Roman Catholic doctrine according to which all saving and important knowledge, whether moral, philosophical or doctrinal, must have come down to us from a primitive revelation given by God when he first created man. So strict traditionalism, as taught by Bonald and Lammenais, tries to avoid the paradox of the beginning of Tradition by denying that any human being has ever been creative in any really important matter. Pope Pius IX, however, was reportedly not quite so pessimistic. According to him, not every human being is divinely destined to be an airhead: no, there is at least one person who has something really important to teach the rest of humanity. 'Sono la tradizione' (I am tradition) he declared, meaning in effect that the teaching office of the Papacy is the sole appointed channel through which Tradition comes into expression.

However, as everyone knows, at the very centre of the Christian tradition stands a man named Jesus. At the liturgy passages from the Synoptic Gospels are still read in which Jesus freely overrides or modifies traditional teachings, and sharply criticizes those power-hungry religious professionals whose exactions burden and distort the religious life of the common people. He seems to have been strongly anti-traditionalist, a religious critic of objectified and professionalized religion.

In religion there is no doubt that the combination of patriarchal government and mindless traditionalism is very, very stultifying. So stultifying, in fact, that most people, most of the time, fail to notice even the most glaring and violent contradictions within their own tradition. It is believed as a matter of dogma that the whole of tradition totalizes into a metaphysical unity as perfect and simple as the very mind of God himself; and where that belief is held it acts to prevent people from noticing the many tensions, conflicts and differences within their own tradition.

Against this background, one can now see that in a sense there has always been radical theology. The creative individuals who initiated and who later enriched the tradition must themselves have been radicals, who criticized and departed from whatever tradition they received. And the newly-developing tradition itself always contains conflicts and tensions, which have a way of prompting later generations of radicals to point out (for example) the gap between the creativity of the founders of Tradition and the sterility of the Tradition that appeals to them.

A conservative theologian, then, is a political loyalist. He strengthens the community and confirms the power of the hierarchy, by defending the unity and perfection of Tradition. By contrast, a radical theologian is perceived as disloyal and subversive. By pointing out conflicts within Tradition, he weakens the authority of the hierarchy and the morale of the entire community. The religious ideal is a state of unthinking harmony: sobornost, the consensus fidelium. The radical theologian who provokes thought and debate is therefore always seen as a troublemaker.

Because the Christian tradition is so eclectic, loosely synthesizing many different strands of thought, it has always been argumentative and internally disputatious. The development of critical thinking in the West around the time of the Reformation made Christianity even more obsessively self-critical and internally disputatious than it was already, to such an extent that many observers have concluded that whereas self-critical thinking is certainly very good for science, it is very bad for religion, and has perhaps fatally weakened Christianity.

This prompts a series of questions. First, how far by now has the radical spirit of doubt, self-questioning and demand for reform spread from Christianity to other faiths? Secondly, how much good has radical theology actually done in Christianity, since the Reformation and since the Enlightenment? And thirdly and finally, are the traditionalists right when they say that religion and traditionalism are one and the same, and that insofar as radical theology succeeds in undermining Tradition it is simply eliminating religion from the world altogether?

In reply to the first of these questions, it seems that—at least since Spinoza—the Jews have tried quite as often and as hard as Christians to work out and to establish a thoroughly criticized and modernized version of their own faith. But in both traditions the bulk of people, so far as they remain practisers of religion at all, remain orthodox. The liberals and the radical modernizers have not yet fully won the argument.

Something similar has to be said of the Hindu tradition, where between 1814 and 1948 a string of energetic reformers and modernizers, from Roy and Sen to Ramakrishna and Gandhi, strove to transform Hinduism into a modern world religion. Fifty years ago, their achievement looked very great; but today one is rather impressed by the way conservative village Hinduism clings on tenaciously, right up to the moment of its own sudden wipe-out by the violent postmodernization of the whole culture. The modernizers did not fully win, and perhaps they couldn't.

It is arguable that Buddhism is the religious tradition that has been most-successfully reformed. A combination of long-established syncretism with recent violent political and cultural upheavals has had the effect of very severely weakening Buddhism in its ancient homelands, whilst at the same time reformed and purified versions of Mahayana Buddhism are now spreading rapidly in the West. However, on the downside it has to be said that, like Christianity, Buddhism has tended also to export to the mission-field its ethnic varieties, its sects and its rival traditions. Perhaps for this reason, the West that receives Buddhism has so far tended to consign it to the counter-culture, amongst the jungle of 'Alternatives.'

As for Islam, it is well-known that a very long line of reforming, syncretistic and modernizing movements, from the Sikhs to the Baha'i, has arisen especially on Islam's eastern borders since the sixteenth century. Yet the main body of Muslims have tended always to expel such movements, and to resist reform. Like traditionalists everywhere they tend to reason that since their religious system is a divinely-revealed and perfect totality, ideas of reform and modernization are simply out of place. Islam doesn't need to be reformed; it needs only to be put into practice.

In sum: since the end of the Middle Ages, there have been many modernizing and reforming movements in the faiths, across the entire Old World. They usually began, in mediaeval times, as democratic or mystical movements of personal devotion. They might then go on to criticize priestcraft, to seek universality, and perhaps to try to break with traditionalism. The Baha'is even proclaimed the equality of the sexes. But nowhere has such a movement yet fully achieved its aims. Everywhere the dominant group, the majority, continues to be of the 'Orthodox,' patriarchal and traditionalist persuasion. After each successive modernizing movement has spent its force, a kind of cultural and institutional drag always tends to bring back the old rituals, the old ways of thinking and the old power-relations.

I conclude that, at any rate until the 1960s, there was a very strong case for saying that, although one can understand why there is radical theology, one can also understand that it will never succeed in its aims. Of course every great religious tradition is a jumble of conflicting elements and strands, and of course every great religious tradition, purporting as it does to represent to us the wisdom of the past, is bound to be somewhat out of date. But people are like that, culture is like that, and language itself is like that. The radical theologian makes the same sort of mistake as the crusader for spelling reform or Esperanto. The cause may indeed be reasonable; but it is quite certainly hopeless.

So one might have said, with some confidence, until about thirty years ago. But then one began to grasp that a new global technological culture had arrived at last, and was beginning to change everything. Based on a girdle of satellites around the Earth, modem communications systems are not only instantaneous, world-wide and cheap: they have huge carrying capacity, and it now seems evident that computers can in principle perform any task that can be precisely defined, and an increasing number that cannot, as well.

Very rapid economic change is one effect of all this. Another is the cultural change that is forced when closed political systems and religious outlooks are blown open by gales of new information. The effect is that every ancient and protected local certainty comes to an end. Instead, every meaning and every truth, all beliefs and values and customs, now begin to float on a globalized free market. Everything has been permanently destabilized. The first major effect of all this was the collapse of East European communism at the end of the 1980s. But we have seen nothing yet. Far bigger collapses than that are now impending—and especially, the breakdown of all the oldest, greatest, best organized and most authoritarian religious systems.

In the case of the collapse of the communist regimes, two factors collaborated. The government could no longer control the spread of information by computers, copying-machines and the like; but, and at least equally serious, there was also an internal decline of faith in the system even amongst the very people who were operating it, and themselves had most to gain by continuing to believe in it. Compare that with what has happened to the Catholic Church in Spain since the death of Franco in 1975, and one begins to grasp the huge scale of the collapse of traditional religion that now impends.

It is curious that in the past thirty or forty years we have become quite accustomed to the idea that environmental disaster impends, and that we need to start changing our ways and planning ahead; but we are very unreceptive to the idea that for many of the same reasons an even bigger religious and cultural disaster impends. We are living in denial. Traditionalism itself encourages the denial of major historical change. Religious leaders spend their mornings in the office managing the rapid downsizing of organized religion, and their evenings moving slowly and gracefully about at religious gatherings in order to give the public impression that there are no reasons whatever for any doubt, anxiety or thought. Everything is as it always was and ever shall be. All is well.

So traditionalism makes denial a way of life—and inadvertently gives to radical theology its new agenda. Because tradition always tries to picture itself as timelessly true, it is systematically unable to think clearly either its own beginning or its own death. But—as T. J. J. Altizer more than anyone else has tried to show us—we live at a time when radical theology is called upon to think not only the Death of God, but also the Birth of God. In the long historical life of Tradition, little of any great intellectual interest can take place. But if Tradition had an historical origin, there must have been pure creative religious thought at its beginning, and pure creative religious thought must be the most exalted, powerful and historically influential thinking there is. And if Tradition is now dying, then radical theology's task is to reopen the awesome possibility of pure creative religious thought. As Elias Canetti puts it, somewhere in his notebooks: "Everything must be reinvented." Yes, indeed: that is what has to be done.

There have already been some indications, both in philosophy and in art, of what must happen. As early as the late 1880s, in their last creative years, Nietzsche and Van Gogh showed independently just how fiercely the fire must burn. The subsequent Modern movement in painting was vividly aware, both that it was trying to reinvent everything, and that this terrible, consuming ambition had a religious character. And one might say that the long conflict between Modernism and 'the general public' was and still is a conflict over the definition of religion. To the general public it seems obvious that religion and traditionalism are one and the same thing. Religion is acceptance and resignation, religion is to be content to recycle for ever a fixed canon of truths, values, symbols and customs. But to the Modernist, religion is an attempt to reinvent everything, an attempt for the sake of which one must live in a state of solar conflagration, burning up, burning out.

I am suggesting, then, that everything that human beings have lived by for the past few millennia is now disappearing down a black hole. We are not wholly unprepared for this moment, because many of our extant religious traditions include some consideration of it. They have retained in their language at least some talk of death. Nothingness, Emptiness, the Void, and universal destruction, perhaps because they were themselves born out of such a time as we now face. Maybe the tradition that we have parroted so unthinkingly for so long does still preserve, in this vocabulary, a faint after-echo, a useful memory, of the Big Bang with which it began.

Radical theology today, then, is called upon to attempt pure creative religious thought: a fresh start. Such thinking is possible. There is in it the greatest joy and exaltation that a human being can know. And there is in it also a consuming fire that the thinker cannot quench. Religious thought is the dance of Siva: it is both creation and destruction. And it is what we all have to attempt: radical theology has suddenly become ecumenical.

4

AFTER LIBERALISM (1990)

Until not very long ago theology and the religious scene generally were dominated by the conflict between conservatives and liberals. It was a dispute with ramifications extending far beyond the English-speaking world, and indeed far beyond Christendom. The question at issue was how far traditional religious ways of thinking could or should change in response to the Enlightenment.

There had of course been a period of Enlightenment previously in the Western tradition, during classical antiquity. In that period Enlightened intellectuals who concerned themselves with religion had already explored many of the options available to them—fideism, allegorism, nature-mysticism, syncretism, introvertive or negative mysticism and so forth. But classical antiquity was not democratic, and the Enlightened mentality was a predominantly literary phenomenon, confined to a smallish minority of the population. At first the modern Enlightenment, beginning in early Renaissance Italy, was also a minority affair. The immense power of a persecuting Church obliged it to be relatively discreet and low-key until the late seventeenth century. But then it began to spread rapidly. Democratic and historicist ideologies developed, claiming that before long everyone was going to go over to the Enlightenment mentality. Laws of historical development made the progressive, and ultimately the complete, secularization of culture unstoppable. To survive, it seemed that religion must change. It must come to terms with Enlightenment.

Accepting all this, and being themselves at least half-Enlightened, the liberals set about reshaping religion to make it more humanistic, democratic, progressive and rational. After Descartes the touchstone of truth tended to be located within the subjectivity of the Enlightened individual. The highest court of appeal was the free individual's reason, conscience and experience. So in liberal religion faith duly became more internalized, with more emphasis upon the human Jesus, upon personal religious experience and upon moral action to reform and improve society. In place of the old passive supernaturalism which saw God as having already fully prescribed the whole framework within which human life must be lived, so that nobody but God could bring about any major change in the human condition, it now came to be held that we human beings are historical agents, called upon ourselves to change our world. The Christian individual was invited to join with others in the great work of building the Kingdom of God on earth. This was a christianized version of the contemporary secular ideologies of historical progress. The liberal God was an inspiring moral ideal, a moral providence perhaps, a side-of-the-angels for us to be on, and the goal of the whole historical process; but he was no longer quite the admonitory voice in one's head, the transcendent cosmic Lord, the dreadful Judge and the loving Heavenly Father of the conservatives. He just wasn't quite so vivid as he had been. The liberal view of God was no more than semi-realist, at least so far as divine personality and divine interventions in the world were concerned. Yet in other respects, as many people will have noticed, the liberals are usually found to be determined and tenacious realists. They still stand in the old platonic tradition, and believe both in one-truth-out-there and in moral-standards-out-there. They are almost without exception scientific realists, and also social-historical optimists who believe, like John Robinson, if not quite in a guaranteed final historical triumph of the good, then at least in a constant Love-out-there at the root of things. And they use a good deal of traditional vocabulary.

The consequence of this has been that throughout the hundred years and more of sharp conservative-versus-liberal controversy, much though the two sides might dislike each other, they were in many ways still talking the same language. They were frenemies, despite the fact that conservative religion has remained so determinedly medieval (or, in the case of orthodox Calvinism, in a very distinctive manner, post-medieval) in its vocabulary and ways of thinking. Religious truth was cosmic-political. We human beings, it was thought, are lost unless our life is anchored and held steady within an immovable framework of objective divine authority, divine law and divine truth. The conservative cosmology is an upward extension of social authority, sacred, hierarchized and animistic. Conservatives lack, or claim to lack, the Enlightened type of consciousness and for the sake of the social order take pains to ensure that they shall go on lacking it, and they view the humanism and the 'laxity', or charitableness, of the liberals with abhorrence.

Yet sharp though the conflict between them could be, I am suggesting that old-style conservatives and liberals seem in retrospect to have been on pretty much the same side and talking much the same language. The conservatives were ironical enough to have themselves at least a tincture of the Enlightenment mentality (enough to enable them to direct their attacks against it accurately), and the liberals were only half-Enlightened anyway because there was still so much realism left in their theories of knowledge and morality. So beneath the superficial disagreements it is not difficult to detect areas of continuing agreement. Conservatives tend to operate in terms of binary oppositions, whereas liberals are usually universalists. Conservatives tend to believe both in Heaven and in Hell whereas liberals hope for universal redemption, but both parties believe in an otherworldly salvation after death. Conservatives tend to take a realistic view of miracles such as the Resurrection, whereas liberals interpret them in more 'spiritual' terms, but both parties believe in 'the myth of the normative Origin.' The liberals may refer back to Jesus' consciousness, his character and the early Christian experience of him, whereas the conservatives refer back to propositions and prodigies, but both continue to appeal to the origins of Christianity as authoritative. Conservatives see sin in more ritual terms, and liberals in more social-moral, but both parties go on using the word. And in general, the conservatives did not by their behaviour seriously threaten the liberals' belief in reason, because the two parties were after all able to reason with each other.

In Britain there are still old-style religious liberals and old-style conservatives, bickering cosily in bed together as they have done for so long. But, I want to suggest, during the 1980s we witnessed their dispute turning into a new and altogether less cosy battle, that between the post-moderns and the fundamentalists. To use Jean Baudrillard's useful term, post-modernism maybe seen as the ecstatic form of Enlightenment, and fundamentalism is certainly the ecstatic form of religious conservatism. With the end of realism in our century, the loss of all objective bearings, and the steady erosion of the distinction between the real and the fictional, everything tends to be transformed into an excessive, hyperbolical and superreal version of itself; and both post-modernism and fundamentalism are ecstatic in this sense. As we saw in the Salman Rushdie affair, the two mentalities are still preoccupied with each other—but now, they are locked in mortal conflict. For whereas old-style religious liberals and conservatives had some sort of reciprocal understanding, there can be no accord between post-modern and fundamentalist believers. Those who look in one direction see only blaspheming nihilism, and those who look the other way see only absolutist fanaticism. Each seems like a damned soul to the other. Both have gone over the top.

This total breakdown of communication is fatal to the old liberal belief—today associated especially with Jurgen Habermas—in the possibility through dialogue of achieving universal and complete mutual comprehension. Who today can think that possible? But then, in recent years the liberal creed has been failing article by article. The belief in 'clean' and uncontaminated data of experience by which to check theories, the belief in self-present, self-scanning and undeceived individual consciousness, the belief in universal moral and intellectual standards, the belief in the distinctions between the real and the fictional and between fact and interpretation, the belief in the progressive historical growth of both consciousness and freedom, the belief that language can be used to tell the truth, the whole truth and nothing but the truth.... And when everything is seen to be invented and the belief in truth is recognised to be only a highly-desirable fiction, then Enlightenment passes completion and begins to turn back upon itself and devour itself. There is no longer anything left in the name of which we are entitled to set out to deprive other people of their fictions. In any case, do we not often nowadays catch ourselves envying other people the fictions they live by? Why be demythologized? Thus Enlightenment in recent years has seen through even itself, and in becoming hyperbolical has lost all grounds for thinking of its own point of view as being in some sense privileged. So the reflexive difficulties into which it has got itself have transfigured it into its ecstatic form, post-modernism. Nihilistic, self-sceptical, super-enlightenment.

Now, as in the 1840s among the Young Hegelians, the question of religion is the heart and centre of the whole affair. If during these past few years you have watched the difficulties of Enlightenment as from outside and with a certain malicious satisfaction, then you are surely gravitating towards fundamentalism. And indeed, is it not obvious today that in the most advanced countries millions of people are reverting with almost-audible relief to a pre-modern mentality? But if on the other hand you have in recent years experienced the difficulties of Enlightenment as darkness and travail within your own soul and as epochal religious events, then you will be sympathetic to the new post-modern theologies now appearing.

The difference is something like this: post-modern religion is religion that fully accepts that it is just human, being made of human signs, and which after having gone through the fires of nihilism knows that it must now continually remake itself as art. And indeed, post-modern religious faith is very close in spirit to present-day painting and writing. By contrast, fundamentalist religion is religion that has glimpsed but has repressed as intolerable and unendurable the knowledge of its own humanness. It has glimpsed nihilism because, of course, it arose precisely out of and in sharp reaction against Darwinism and the later Victorian crisis of faith. So to that extent it really does know the alternative. Its brief glimpse into the abyss has given to it its sense of urgency. It clutches at authority, charisma, tradition and certainty. It desperately needs to think of religious ideas and religious truth as divinely-given, fearsome and uncriticizable. As everyone who has ever belonged to a fundamentalist or ultra-conservative religious group will know, the group goes to great lengths to exclude unwelcome questioning. Literature is controlled, members must speak in stock phrases and have stock experiences, religious meanings are insistently assumed to be univocal, critical reflection is implicitly (and therefore doesn't need to be explicitly) ruled out, and individual deviance is sensed and dealt with instantly. All this bears painful and eloquent testimony to the intensity of people's fear of the abyss, and the high price they are ready to pay to be shielded from it.

By contrast, post-modern religion thinks that we need to train ourselves to look steadily at the abyss. In fact, the message of both Christianity and Buddhism (Die to the self! and There is no self!) is that to gaze steadfastly into the Void purges us of anxious egoism, and liberates us for love and creativity. There are plenty of hints of this in the religious tradition: the Wholly Other, the Absurd, the Sea without a shore, the Divine Darkness, the Dark Night of the Soul, the incomprehensibility of God, dying with Christ. You must collide with something unthinkable that unselfs you, and it is the Nihil. Poetically speaking, the abyss is merciful and gracious. It puts us to death and raises us to life again.

Old-style liberal religion was reluctant to let go completely. It clung to at least semi-realism about God, the objective world and moral value. Post-modern religion is ecstatic liberalism in that it insists upon letting go. It says: Nothing is sacrosanct, everything is revisable. There's nothing out there or in here, and we should be truly beliefless. It is spiritually liberating to be free-floating, and to regard all religious ideas as being human and therefore open to criticism and revision. To hold on is to risk falling into superstition and fanaticism. The peculiar sort of poise, strength and sanity that religion can give is only to be had if the full price is paid; one must embrace the Void.

Here, there is undoubtedly a considerable gap between the older liberals and the newer radicals and post-modernists. In the language of William James, the liberals were once-born types. Their outlook was in general kindly and optimistic, their universe solid, comfortable and well-furnished. But they now seem dated. Liberalism is being squeezed out, in society, in the Church and in the intellectual world. Western thought has been getting more and more sceptical for a long time. The main theme is very simple: it is the realization that our knowledge-systems, our beliefs, our myths, our norms, our meanings, even our values, are as human and local and transient as we are. That is the thought that freezes the blood. The older liberalism could not bear it, and turned away. But the post-liberal sort of theology I have been trying to describe will be nihilistic. It will head determinedly into the darkness. It knows that Western religious thought now needs to turn in a somewhat early-Buddhist direction, and it claims that in doing so it will not become any less Christian. Quite the contrary. We are talking about renewal.

5

LEARNING TO LIVE WITHOUT 'IDENTITY' (1997)

Is it now too late to be talking about Jewish-Christian dialogue? As it is usually understood, the phrase implies cautious, friendly conversations or negotiations between teams of somewhat elderly parties, mostly male, who represent two independent communities of faith. The aim is to find some common ground and to establish amicable relations—in short, to agree to differ, because it is tacitly taken for granted that the two communities propose to remain permanently distinct. We are coming together in order to agree upon how we can most peaceably stay apart. On neither side is there expected to be any compromise whatever, because it is taken for granted that religious allegiance is like allegiance to one's own nation, but even more so. It is both what people call an 'identity', and what people call an 'absolute'. That seems to mean that through it, uniquely, we identify ourselves, finding our place in the world and our task in life; and that therefore its moral claim upon us overrides all other claims. Accordingly, negotiations between representatives of different religious groups are rather like diplomatic negotiations between the representatives of distinct sovereign nation-states. The talks may lead to the establishment of peaceful, friendly and co-operative relations between two sovereign parties. But sovereignty itself remains axiomatically non-negotiable. It is an absolute, a unique 'identity', almost an eternal essence, something that one cannot envisage ever being superseded or becoming obsolete. Its claims are a matter of life and death. For their sake one must be ready to accept martyrdom, or even (nowadays) to get involved with terrorism.

This ancient idea of unconditional allegiance to some local group is still found in many forms in the late-modern world. It may be called fundamentalism, tribalism, communalism, ethnonationalism, and so on; and it creates a rather untidy picture of the human scene. The local god, or nation, or other object of unconditional allegiance to which people rally may be almost any threatened language, or ethnic group, or 'race', or religious group, or nation state; and the domains of these varied rival foci of 'absolute' allegiance may very easily overlap, and so create acute and painful conflicts in the minds of individuals.

Now I have a number of arguments to put forward in connection with this situation. Their cumulative effect is, I shall suggest, that we should give up the received quasi-political and highly reifying ways of thinking about 'the Synagogue' and 'the Church', and the dialogue between them. The very

41

notion of 'a religion' as a small, distinct, unchanging, self-identical, closed ideological world, like an isolated sovereign nation, in which people are unanimous in matters of belief, is dead. Notoriously, we can't even say very clearly exactly who 'the Jews' are nowadays, or who might count as their officially-accredited and generally-recognized representatives. There are too many shades of lapsed membership and partial belief. And much the same is true of 'Christianity' and 'the Church'. I shall argue that the real situation is that if we want to go on thinking of 'Judaism' and 'Christianity' as distinct traditions, each with its own literature, its own body of beliefs, its character-istic style, then we should recognize that they are nowadays fast becoming entities like 'Platonism'. As their embodiment in a distinct community of shared belief becomes ever less clear-cut, they are becoming assimilated. They are turning into relatively enduring and identifiable strands within an historically-evolving global cultural tradition. As such, they are no longer strictly tied to just one territory or organisation: they are becoming public property, freely accessible to everyone, and part of everyone's thinking. In this sense, I am myself as Jewish as many Jews, and as much a Buddhist as many Buddhists. Nowadays, surely, we all of us 'contain multitudes'.

A great tradition eventually comes to belong to all humankind. When, not long ago, the site of Aristotle's Lyceum was found in Athens, local politicians declared grandiloquently that the remains 'bear witness to the continuity of Hellenic civilization', with the implication that they see them-selves as the true and legitimate heirs and successors of Pericles and Plato. But in practice people around the world seem to feel able to study Plato and Aristotle for themselves, without needing to seek instruction from mod-ern Greek politicians and philosophers. And similarly, it has become very noticeable in recent years that the best writing about Christianity no longer comes from Christians, nor even from traditional academic theologians. It comes from post-Christians, and has done so for many years, because mod-ern Christians have come down somewhat since the days of their own great tradition, just as modern Greeks and Egyptians are not quite the equals of their ancient predecessors. In which case we should perhaps think of giv-ing up the idea that 'Christians', 'Muslims' and 'Jews' are three very distinct communities rather like nation-states, each with privileged access to its own unchanging core-tradition of religious and moral wisdom. Until about the sixteenth century something like that was indeed the case: if you wanted to learn about another major tradition, then you had to travel and to sit at the feet of a learned person from within that tradition. But nowadays abundant printed books, the free worldwide dissemination of information, and the globalisation of culture have made everything freely available to everyone. We can now be anything and everything. Most of us, at least, are not con-fined, and do not wish to be confined, to a cultural or religious sub-world or ghetto. Judaism and Christianity, like Platonism and Buddhism, are becoming strands in everyone's thinking. The old idea of an exclusive and unchanging historically-transmitted religious 'identity'—a unique body of truth in the sole custody of a special body of people—is rapidly becoming obsolete.

Is it not curious that the people who are chosen to represent us in ecumenical and inter-faith conversations always turn out to be very cautious and conservative characters who think like lawyers? In a world in which tradition is dying, we seem to feel safest when we are represented by extreme traditionalists. We like to be represented by people who are utterly unrepresentative of us. It is as if we very much want them to go on defending, on our behalf, positions that we no longer hold ourselves.

What then has happened? In the earliest times—or so we are told—religion was monocultural and henotheistic. Each people or *ethne* had their own language, their own sacred territory and their own god. Identities were clear-cut to such an extent that if you went to live in another territory, amongst another people, those new people became your people and their god your god. (See Ruth 1:15f.; 1 Samuel 26:19 etc.) The notion that religion is—or at least ideally should be—strictly ethnic and territorial has survived to this day. People still use terms like Christendom and Islam in a territorial way, and speak of lands like France and Italy as 'Roman Catholic countries'. Politicians in those countries do not find it at all easy to acknowledge publicly the fact that there may very soon be—and perhaps already are—more practising Muslims than practising Catholics in the home population. In Italy some years ago, politicians who were not themselves practising Catholics at all nevertheless found they simply could not bring themselves to attend the inauguration of Rome's first major mosque. They were accustomed to thinking of themselves as non-Catholics in a Catholic country, and somehow could not take in the thought that they might be turning into non-Muslims in a Muslim country.

Our thinking about true religion and territoriality has become oddly confused. For more than one-and-a-half millennia the Jews were in effect the principal and most obvious example of an ancient faith that had lost its own territory and now survived within Christendom, within Islam, and elsewhere in encapsulated form. People identified themselves as Jews, and were identified, in every other way except through their possession of their own holy land. Your Jewishness was conveyed to you through your genealogy, your community-membership, your language, scriptures, customs and cultural tradition: but territory—no. The Jews were often regarded as a dispersed, homeless, fugitive people, living in a state of what seemed permanent diaspora, homelessness. The state of being exiled from one's proper sacred territory seemed pitiable. Then came the Restoration, the founding of the state of Israel, and a seemingly wonderful fulfilment of prophecy. But, fifty years later, not all Jews have wished to return, and visitors to Israel are astonished to find what a secular society it is, and how little regard is paid to the Torah. Can Judaism not survive the fulfilment of its own hopes? Is the recovered possession of one's own holy land somehow now a religiously bad thing? In countries like the United States there has for some time been anxiety that the Jews in diaspora may disappear within half a century by marrying-out, and by complete assimilation into the host culture. But now we find that a worse danger threatens in the opposite direction: the Return to Israel fulfills Judaism—and then eclipses it, as all the precious old religious values of Judaism disappear into militant nationalist politics.

Judaism, then, seems to be caught between Scylla and Charybdis. In America, and in 'the West' generally, it threatens to become just one more strand in the new globalized world-historical culture, like Platonism. It will become simply part of the universal syllabus, part of everybody's heritage, and will no longer be, nor need to be, embodied in a distinct visible human society. At the opposite extreme, Judaism also disappears in Israel. The ancient dream of a mono-ethnic theocratic state society cannot be realized in the modern world, except by turning religious values into political ones.

Islam is, of course, nowadays caught in just the same dilemma; and so is Christianity. The ideal of 'a Christian country' is fading, disappearing. In Western society at large, 'the Christian tradition' has become just one more strand in everybody's cultural heritage. What survives of 'the Church' is so drastically reduced that it no longer has any special claim to, nor expertise in, the old 'great' tradition. In which case, conversations between officially-nominated teams of Jewish and Christian representatives will be mainly exercises in denial. They will be conducted as if old-style distinct, homogeneous faith communities, in which traditional religious values are preserved intact, still exist—which is not the case, in a world where all of us alike are 'mediatized', immersed in the new media culture. And so long as we go on clinging to the memory of our lost closed worlds, for so long we will be failing to discuss the prospect that faces us all alike—both people who are ancestrally Jewish, and people who are ancestrally Christian—in the new globalized world-culture. At our interfaith conversations we try to reassure ourselves that we really are still different from each other and do still possess our own distinct 'identities'. But the reality is that the process of world-cultural assimilation is swallowing us both up. We are becoming more and more alike. All distinct ethnic and religious identities, of the old kind that we are so desperately nostalgic for, are rapidly vanishing.

This very painful example brings out the scale of today's religious crisis. We are right to have seen the Jews as 'a light to the nations', because certain universal structures of religious thought have been so clearly and even classically exemplified for us all by the Jews for so long. The central idea is that of a domain unified under a Monarch, a transcendent controlling principle and focus of loyalty that has instituted and now orders everything. The Monarch's power unifies everything and makes it all holy: the Holy Land, the Holy People, the sacred language, the Holy Books of the Law. There is a very clear line between the sacred and profane realms, and it is the line that separates insiders from outsiders; and all your various loyalties—to your people, to your mother-tongue, to your land, to your holy city, to your God and so on—are fully synthesized.

Some such arrangement as this prevailed for most of the time around the world from the beginnings of agricultural civilization until about the year 1500 CE. The Hebrew Bible describes with great clarity the (rather late) establishment of Israel's version of the system, and prints it almost indelibly upon our minds and hearts as the ideal to which we aspire. This is what we long for; this is how human beings should live. This is what it is to have an identity; this is what it is to know where you belong, who your friends are and who your enemies, and how you should live.

But it is all fast disappearing now, as I first realised when in 1980 I visited an Inuit (or Eskimo) primary school in Baffin Island and found that the syllabus, the culture, the language and even the pop music being imparted to the children was indistinguishable from that in the primary school which my own younger daughter was still attending in Cambridge. We cling to our old identities—just because they are vanishing so rapidly. Much of religious talk and practice nowadays seems to consist of lamentations over, and rather ineffectual attempts to re-enact, all the things that we are now fast losing. Wouldn't it be better if we were to talk together about what is now coming upon all of us?

For is it not the case that our own tradition itself anticipated the globalization—the reversal of Babel—that we now see? The development of a single world-wide communications network, the emergence of a globally-dominant language, the English language, and the spread of a single ethic, based mainly upon the UN Charter and the Universal Declaration of Human Rights, all around the globe, is surely a very significant religious event. The choice of its motto by the BBC, a lifetime ago, shows that this was once obvious. 'Nation shall speak peace unto nation.' But today, unfortunately, we are absorbed in trying to conserve our separate identities. You have never seen, and I at least have not seen, any recent piece of religious writing that welcomes globalization as Pentecost, as a fulfillment of ancient hopes. Why not? Are we missing something?

Part Two

*Preaching the Non-realist
Doctrine of God*

6

GOD WITHIN (1980)

During these last few weeks there has been a small commotion over a recent book of mine which teaches a version of Christian existentialism. It says that to believe in God is simply freely to impose upon oneself an infinite requirement, the task of becoming spirit. The implications of the thesis are made rather explicit, and the book has been called atheistic. One section of the Church press is praying for me and another, less charitably, is demanding my resignation. So I imagine you may be expecting to hear what I have to say for myself.

The book is called *Taking Leave of God* and is an attempt to write a modern spirituality—a risky business. The title echoes a line from the medieval mystic Meister Eckhart: 'Man's last and highest parting comes when, for God's sake, he takes leave of God.' I understand that to mean that in the end we must give up objectivity and external guarantees, because the highest religious truth is inward. The summit of the religious life is pure spirit without distinction of subject and object.

This introduces the point that the book is a long critique of excessively objectifying or realistic views about God and religious belief. Many people's religious ideas are very literalistic. They think it essential to faith that one should first of all accept a long series of supernatural facts—assertions about supernatural beings and supernaturally-caused events. These supernatural facts, these objective dogmas, are seen as the *sine qua non* of faith. Unless they are true, religion is illusory, and unless you accept them, you are not a believer at all.

I have brought forward many arguments against this idea. One obvious one is that under present conditions it is, to say the least, not easy to establish the truth of even one of these supernatural beliefs. In almost every possible way they are topics of sharp controversy and shrouded in doubt and obscurity. How could we ever rationally commit our whole lives on the basis of such uncertainties? Can it be right to set such strict—and indeed impossible—intellectual conditions for honest entry upon the Christian life?

Put it the other way round and we may ask ourselves: 'Is the Christian life worth living for its own sake?' Surely, 'Yes'. For Christian holiness requires of us purity of heart, inner integrity, active love and complete unselfishness. These qualities of character not only *may* but positively *must be* sought disinterestedly and for their own sakes. But in that case acceptance of the supernatural doctrines and motives cannot be the necessary basis for holiness in quite the way people suppose. Holiness must in the end be pursued for its own sake and be its own reward.

I think people are already seeing this point. In modern times the fear of Hell has suddenly disappeared as a motive for living the Christian life. We no longer seem to need it. It seems that we are already making the transition to a more adult and disinterested religious outlook.

These and other considerations lead me to propose a switch in the way we see religion. I want to put spirituality and the lived life of religion first, and then treat the doctrines as symbolic expressions of the spirituality. I do not say, '*Because* the supernatural doctrines are first descriptively true, *therefore it* makes good sense to live the Christian life.' I say instead that the spirituality, the ethics and the ritual of religion come first. They are what attract us in the first place, and they must be pursued for their own sakes. The doctrines need to be interpreted symbolically. They communicate to us what the religious ideal is and how to attain it. We join in the language of worship by way of pledging our allegiance and deepening our commitment to the Christian life.

So I am led to a symbolist and regulative view of religious truth. God symbolises the religious ideal and its claim upon us and guides us in the spiritual life. I must confess that I am quite uncertain about the objective metaphysical reality of a personal God as a distinct individual being, though the book retains the possibility of a hidden Transcendent God. But so far as the day-to-day life of religion is concerned what I mean by God is something like the Pearl of Great Price, the religious ideal that guides us and is our goal.

At this point I want to introduce the second theme of the book, which is an attempt to synthesise the modern spirituality of liberation with the traditional Christian spirituality.

I mean this: for a long time now the basic drive of modern people has been a struggle for personal freedom and autonomy, a struggle that has involved rebellion against all traditional authorities whether political or religious. People passionately demand liberation and self-possession. They want to control their own lives and they want to become free, self-expressing, fully-conscious spiritual subjects. The ideal is to become fully oneself, in full control of one's own life.

This modern drive for liberation and individual human rights is so strong that the Churches have at least partly endorsed it. Yet it is plainly difficult to reconcile with the traditional Christian outlook. For the language of Christianity is steeped in a masters-and-servants vision of the universe, in which our highest happiness is to serve One above us whose will is our law and our destiny. Traditional Christianity (understood literally) seems to have a colonialist view of man as someone who needs to be ruled from outside by a superior Power, whereas what modern man above all desires is autonomy. Traditional Christianity offers only the discipline of being someone else's servant. It proposed 'the handmaid of the Lord' as the ideal believer.

So is it possible to reconcile Christianity and freedom? Can Christianity offer anything to the modern autonomous person in his or her quest for liberation? On my account, 'Yes', for I emphasise that religious commitment must be a free and self-imposed acceptance of the religious demand for holiness, our own highest spiritual fulfilment. God's call to holiness *exactly* coincides with my will to freedom.

In support, I point to the theme of internalisation in the Bible. Instead of being constrained by an external Law that cannot save, people will be filled with a new spirit. Hearts of stone will be replaced by hearts of flesh. The external Temple and external circumcision will be replaced by inward equivalents. The movement from Letter to Spirit, outward to inward, is a powerful biblical theme.

I have also used the phrase 'Christian Buddhism'. I do not mean that I am a Buddhist. I just mean that Buddhism is an inner discipline, it stresses autonomy, and it exalts spirituality above theological doctrine. Similarly, I would like to see Christians turn away from their obsessive attempts to convince themselves and others about objective supernatural facts. Even if we had them I do not think they would really help much—and I do not really think we can get them. Instead, more attention should be paid to ethics and spirituality, for religious truth is in the end subjective, not objective.

At any rate, I attempted in the book to achieve a *tour de force,* a synthesis of the spirit of Christianity with the spirit of freedom, so that a fully-secular person might think it possible to pursue the Christian path to sanctity for its own sake. It was a bold idea—perhaps too bold. Some people are dismissing it as merely destructive, as atheism, and in general as of no value. If they are right, then it's back to the drawing-board for me. I tried to demythologise dogma into spirituality and to claim that the spirituality can be pursued for its own sake. I looked for an undogmatic Christian faith. If I was wrong, then it should at least be noted that the problems I was trying to deal with still remain to be solved.

In closing, I should add that I love Christian prayer and worship. But I think it vital to see that the language of worship is poetic and expressive rather than technical and descriptive. Worship is a way of acting out and deepening our commitment to the Christian life and it teaches us spiritual values in symbolic language. In former days people used the language of myth and symbolism with unconscious ease. But nowadays critical thinking makes us aware of the merely metaphorical and human character of our own ideas, in religion as in other matters. This new self-awareness has involved a certain fall from innocence, but it cannot be helped, and I am arguing that we can profit from it.

However, since I am so cautious about all doctrinal questions I cannot have any very strong itch to undermine other people's convictions. So if what I have said has offended you, disregard it. Just allow me to say that for the people of the Bible the commitment of the will to the new life of personal integrity and unselfish love was at least a very large part of faith. In Jesus' name. Amen.

7

MAKE BELIEVE (1982)

Galatians 5.1: 'For freedom Christ has set us free; stand fast therefore, and do not submit again to a yoke of slavery.'

The New Testament epistles often make a contrast between two kinds of religion. There is a religion of the letter and a religion of the Spirit. There is a religion of milk fed to babes in Christ, and there is a religion of meat for adults who are old enough to think and act for themselves. There is a religion for schoolboys who are under the discipline of an external authority, and there is a religion for sons who have come of age and entered upon their inheritance. There is a religion of external commandments and there is an inward religion of freedom. Sometimes St Paul is contrasting the Old Covenant with the New, and sometimes he is making a distinction between two stages in the personal development of each Christian believer. It was evidently very important to him that Christians should be satisfied with nothing less than the full maturity and freedom of the gospel, and should not allow siren voices to lure them back into immature and authoritarian styles of religion.

The issue St Paul raises is still alive. Through all the history of the church the battle for the full freedom of the gospel has had to be waged ceaselessly and has never been decisively won. The struggle for change and renewal has continued, but it has always been opposed by the forces of tradition which seek to restore pre-Christian structures and ways of thinking.

On the one hand, it is an obvious historical fact that Christianity lives by continual change. The gospel is not something that can be passed from one person to another unexamined, like an unopened parcel. On the contrary, the very nature of religious truth is that it must be continually rediscovered and reminted. The gospel is not a static ideology, but a life that continually renews itself. Each believer must discover it for the first time, and each theologian must begin all over again. The pattern is that each succeeding Christian thinker and innovator frames his position and constructs some sort of pedigree for it by means of which he ties it into the received tradition. In this way the Christian tradition accumulates like a string of onions. Nothing runs the whole length of the string, but the continual fresh starts, each duly tied in to the chain, produce an impression of continuity. It is only when you look closely that you realize that the tradition is entirely made up of fresh starts that have subsequently been woven together to create the effect of an unbroken line.

But, on the other hand, this task of continual recreation and renewal always runs into opposition, and has to be undertaken in the teeth of a good deal of misunderstanding. The reason is that people find it hard to accept that Christianity lives by continual death and rebirth. They keep falling back upon a pre-Christian conception of faith as concerned with what is fixed, authoritative and unchanging. They need at least an illusion of immutability. So there is a constant popular pressure for immobilism and unthinking dogmatism.

This pressure for immobility can be very damaging. To take a minor illustration of it, out in the parishes the laity often tend to have very fixed role-expectations about the behaviour of the clergyman. They require him to behave and to speak in prescribed ways, and profess to be very shocked and indignant if he does not act in just the way that their expectations dictate. This pressure can be psychologically very damaging, and from a Christian point of view can destroy all spontaneity, humanity and freedom. It is important not to allow oneself to succumb to it.

In a rather similar way, theologians may be pressed by people's expectations to think certain things and to speak in certain ways. In this case, the reason is that people's perception of religious meanings tends to be very fixed and unquestioned. However, the task of the creative theologian is to attempt to bring about appropriate changes in people's perception of religious meanings, and this is inevitably a very difficult thing to do. Any shift in religious meanings is felt to be very threatening. People feel that they are losing something old and familiar, and neither understand nor welcome what they are being offered in its place. So there is trouble. Especially since 1830, almost all creative theologians have attracted criticism in both the Roman Catholic and the Protestant traditions. The same public controversies have been replayed over and over again.

In some cases, progress does seem to be made. In 1860 a modest and rather boring symposium called *Essays and Reviews* was published in Britain. It was a very moderate plea for liberalism in theology. The essayists were accused of atheism and of moral dishonesty in retaining their Orders, and there was an immense outcry and a series of court cases which continued for several years. Yet one of the essayists survived to become, thirty years later, Archbishop of Canterbury. This was one of those cases where the heresy of one generation became the orthodoxy of the next, the sort of case that Jesus described as 'whitewashing the tombs of the prophets'.

So progress can slowly be made, but meanwhile the pressure towards conformity and immobility remains strong. One must continue to struggle against it, because otherwise—as one of the 1860 essayists said—the church will 'die from the top'. In the past, Christian faith has always lived by the law of death and rebirth, and has struggled to renew itself in each succeeding period. Even today the same task must be attempted. We must try to articulate Christian faith in a fully modern idiom for our own age.

But the difficulties are very great today, because of the wholly exceptional magnitude and rapidity of cultural change in the modern period. If faith is to become fully contemporary and to engage with the spiritual life of our own age, it must undergo yet another mutation. Only, this time, because there is so much ground to make up, the personal cost of winning one's way through to a truly contemporary faith will be greater than ever before, and the opposition will be correspondingly sharper.

For in the modern period the gap between established Christian ways of thinking and the surrounding secular culture has become very wide. Look at it first from within the circle of faith, and we see that for nearly three centuries most major Christian movements have been neo-conservative. The movements that have most lastingly entered into the life of the churches have been, for example, in the eighteenth century, Pietism, Methodism and Evangelicalism; in the nineteenth century, Anglo-Catholicism and Roman Catholic Ultramontanism; and in the twentieth century, Fundamentalism, Pentecostalism and various other neo-conservative movements. Faced with external criticism, the tendency has been to strengthen the defences, reaffirm traditional language, and retreat into a ghetto of the mind. Of course there have been liberalizing and modernizing movements too, and they have enjoyed some successes, but their permanent influence in the church has not been so great as the influence of the neo-conservative movements.

The result, as everyone knows, has been that there has been a widening of the gap between Christian and secular ways of thinking. One consequence of this is that there is a danger of Christian language becoming evacuated of meaning, and being reduced to a series of shibboleths. For example, in the recently-publicized ARCIC conversations, it transpired that many Anglicans feel that there is not enough scriptural evidence for the corporal assumption into heaven of the Blessed Virgin Mary. The question was discussed as if we knew what is meant by a corporal assumption into heaven, and the only issue is whether we have enough evidence for the proposition. But to an educated modern person who is used to examining closely the meanings of words, the real difficulty is that he cannot see what can be meant by an apotheosis, an ascension, or a corporal assumption into heaven. A human body is a spatially extended object. If it moves, it must move along a continuous track through space and time, and for it to remain alive its physical environment must remain stable within very narrow limits. I can go so far as to imagine, I suppose, that Mary's body might suddenly vanish; but I cannot imagine by what means and to what place it is supposed to be transported, or how it lives when it gets there. Of course, by study of the history of religions I can learn about other similar ideas that have been held in various other cultures. I can learn how these ideas worked, and I can produce a sort of sociological interpretation of the function of such beliefs. However, if I conclude that *that* must be the meaning of the doctrine, I am told that my interpretation is heretical. So I am defeated. The language appears to me to be meaningless, except on the basis of cosmological and scientific beliefs that appear to be plainly untenable. The debate between believers who do accept and believers who do not accept the corporal assumption of Mary into heaven thus seems to me to be a meaningless debate, conducted within a sub-culture on the basis of presuppositions that became untenable many centuries ago. I can't take sides, when neither side is saying anything intelligible.

Here, then, is just one example of how religious language, maintained unchanged within the circle of faith, threatens to become quite meaningless. And it shows us why religious conservatism fails. It tries to maintain the integrity of faith uncorrupted by worldly modernizing ways of thinking, and the upshot is that it falls into meaninglessness. The language deteriorates into a series of empty passwords. People go on using these passwords to prove their orthodoxy to each other, but the passwords have in fact become nothing more than empty sounds. And my fear is that by today a very great deal of Christian language has suffered this fate. To quote another example, I receive many letters exhorting me to get acquainted with certain very important invisible persons. But in our world today it is very hard to see how to understand and put to use the idea of an invisible person. Christian language presents so many puzzles that a demanding spiritual quest must now be undertaken if we are to remint Christian meanings. If people tell me that there is a perfectly intelligible and satisfactory orthodox faith and they see no problem with it, then I can only reply, good luck to you; but unfortunately to me it seems that the deterioration of Christian language has now gone so far that I am compelled to go back to square one and try to think it all out again for myself.

For consider now what has been happening outside the walls of the church during all these years. The whole idea of absolute and unquestionable truth, coming down from above and backed by the power of social authority, has gone and has been replaced by a new conception of knowledge. In our culture the only knowledge now recognized is man-made, provisional and critically-established. The only way to truth is by free enquiry. Theories are put forward and tested publicly against evidence not under their control; and they are maintained only until they are falsified or shown to need reformulating. A theory is of interest only in so far as it is formulated precisely and open to some kind of testing. There is no dogmatic knowledge at all any more, for we have found by experience that such real truth as it is given to human beings to attain can be found only by constantly and habitually seeking out and testing all concealed assumptions. The knowledge we get in this way is admittedly merely human, socially constructed, and subject to continual revision, but it is all we have. Nowadays a sceptical presumption pervades all our knowledge, testing it all the time and keeping it continually on the edge of breakdown. Yet this sceptical presumption is also the basis of a new and odd kind of strength. To a traditional dogmatist, used to living with a solid structure, the critical way of life seems intolerable. Living with no fixed framework at all, the critical thinker seems to be a sort of footloose vagrant. Yet critical thinking has produced the fabulously rich and complex world of modern science and all the other structures of knowledge with which a modern university is concerned. Yes, they are fluid and insubstantial by traditional dogmatic standards, yet they are also very beautiful and in their own way very powerful creations.

Now it seems to me that a fully modern Christian faith has to come to terms with the critical spirit. For me that means that modern faith must be pilgrim faith, faith in the open air, faith unprotected by any fixed dogmatic framework, faith that lives by a continual death and rebirth, and is completely open to change. Its course is guided, not by fixed points in the past, but by future ideals that are aimed at. The resources of Christian language and tradition are used not in a dogmatic way, but instrumentally as tools for the furtherance of the spiritual life.

Traditional faith perceives the universe as like a great house with rules laid down and with various tasks to be performed. Finding your vocation meant discovering what function had from all eternity been assigned to you, for you to perform as your contribution to the running of the whole household. With such a world-view, people drew their sense of life's meaning and purpose from above. Religious values and life-tasks were ready-made. You needed only to fit in and to find your pre-ordained place in the whole scheme of things.

That view of the world, typical of a traditional society, has now wholly passed away. We are now in a world where we can no longer be mere passive recipients of meaning, but where we have to create meaning. For we now know that all meanings are human constructions, as in Niels Bohr's quantum physics, where the world is no more than a system of probabilities until theory-guided human observations make it determinate. Or, to take a very different example, different languages and different societies construct reality in different ways. To those who study many religions it is obvious that religion is a facet of culture, a changing social construction, a way of shaping human life. It is only in the modern period that we have come to see how profoundly human activity shapes reality; but once we do realize it then our understanding of faith must become creative. God himself must be thought of, not as a metaphysical being, but rather as the ideal goal of the spiritual life, and the Christian task is to bring into being a world in which people have become fully conscious and liberated creators of religious meaning and value—the world that Jesus called the kingdom of God. If I could summarize the view that I have come to in one sentence, it might go something like this: all the many worlds that human beings have inhabited are now understood to be human social constructions; Christian faith is a corporate commitment to attempt to bring into being the new world proclaimed by the earthly Jesus and symbolized by the exalted Jesus Christ.

In the past it has been common for people to see the religious quest as a quest for a sort of metaphysical underpinning for the present order of things. Religion was concerned with validating authority, and providing cosmological backing for institutions. These ideas are still popular even today, when we see the Pope surrounded by the same sort of ideology as the Pharaoh of Egypt and the Inca of Peru. Sacred authority descends from the heavens through the earthly representative of God, and is then diffused through the various ranks beneath him to the common people. Such ways of thinking are at least five thousand years old, and are evidently still influential: but to my mind they are not really tenable today. For me Christian faith is a project for a new humanity in a new world. It is a spirituality, a way of inner transformation for each believer; and it is a social ethic. It is primarily a religion of redemption. The old realist metaphysical theologies were mainly concerned to guarantee and to validate. Their interest was fundamentally political rather than truly religious. I want to replace that kind of theology with what you might call a theology of ideals, or a theology of hope. The object is not to mobilize religious sentiment around the *status quo* or to seek cosmic reassurance, but to mobilize Christian aspiration after the new humanity and the new world promised in Jesus Christ.

On Saturday next I have a new book appearing called *The World to Come*. It is a fairly tough book, though I hope a little easier to read than the last one. It is mainly concerned with how we are to make the difficult transition from the traditional realist faith to the new fully voluntary and creative kind of faith that I am groping after.

For make no mistake: the transition is difficult, at any rate for most of us, and especially for those of us who have been strongly committed to a realist theology and have felt it slipping away from **us** in the last twenty years. For us—I mean, for people like me—the new kind of faith can only be reached by passing through the fire.

On the other hand, I do know some people who have taken to the new point of view easily and without difficulty. They have never been strongly committed to a metaphysical theology, nor have they suffered from the various psychological hang-ups associated with realist faith. They have always seen religious ideas as symbolic projections that vary from one culture to another, and are to be used simply as tools. They have always regarded Christianity as primarily an ethical and spiritual path, and a project for the renewal of human nature. I've been surprised to find them already living at their ease in a territory which I have been able to reach only after a more arduous journey than I care to recall.

So although *The World to Come* is almost apocalyptically strenuous, I am hopeful that a time may come when the struggle to get free of dogmatic Christianity will be no more than a memory. Christian faith will be intellectually and psychologically purified, and will simply address itself to the task of bringing into being the new age of which we have a promise and a foretaste in our Lord and Saviour Jesus Christ.

8

RELIGIOUS EXPERIENCE (C.1986)

People are strikingly uncritical about their own religious experience. Almost without exception, they take it at face value, seeing it as in a mysterious manner giving them precious undistorted information from a source outside themselves. It is a sort of revelation, and people do not usually think of revelation as having been moulded by history and culture. Yet this assumption that religious experience is an innocent datum is hard to reconcile with the obvious fact that every religious experience turns out to be framed in the local vocabulary and to confirm some current local belief.

More than that, 'religious experience' itself has a history. The phrase was given its modern currency by William James, whose Gifford Lectures, *The Varieties of Religious Experience,* were published in 1902. *The Oxford English Dictionary* and its *Supplement* do not find any earlier use of the precise phrase 'religious experience'. But they remind us that the appeal to experience in religion is as old as British empiricism itself. It dates back at least to the late seventeenth century, to John Owen and the heyday of puritan scholasticism.

Two points in puritan theology are vital to the understanding of why religious experience developed in our culture in the way it did. First, Calvin wanted Scripture alone to be the rule of faith, but was faced with the familiar problem of the diversity of interpretations. Did not this mean that there would always be the need for a powerful central teaching authority to control the interpretation of Scripture, as Rome claimed? Calvin replied that the prayerful and faithful reader of Scripture would be guided to interpret it aright by the inward testimony of the Holy Spirit. No Pope is needed, for God provides an inner guide to Truth. Here, then, we see emerging already in Calvin himself a forerunner of the later Cartesian and Enlightenment belief that objective Truth can be determined within individual subjectivity.

The second way in which puritanism shaped our modern assumptions about religious experience was through its doctrines of irresistible Grace and Assurance. People were frantic for the assurance of salvation. If God's eternal decree is secret, how can I know that I am among the elect? Answer: I can be sure of final salvation if I have personally experienced the compelling power of Grace within my soul. God is almighty and does nothing in vain. If you have ever received Grace, then you may be certain of your own final salvation. And how can you be sure of having actually received it? By the sudden and irresistible force with which it rushes into the soul.

Thus puritanism could lead people to attach great importance to sudden, charismatic religious experiences, especially those which seem the most unmerited, unprepared-for and compulsive. Religious experience is like an orgasm from nowhere, warm and melting—and a very good thing to have, because it is a pledge of final salvation.

The subsequent history of religious experience in the Anglo-Saxon world has continued these themes. For example, if inner religious experience provides a short cut to Truth independent of the teaching authority of the Church, it is not surprising that to this day religious experience should remain so very common outside the churches (see David Hay, *Exploring Inner Space*, 1987, p. 130). Because of the puritan doctrines about election, irresistible Grace and assurance, people still want to view their own religious experiences as suddenly and purely given to them from Above. Because we have such a long tradition of bourgeois individualism and belief in empirical verification, we still to a quite remarkable degree assume that the objective Truth of momentous doctrines and theories can be decided just by events in our own personal psychological history. We Anglo-Saxons resisted Freud for so long because we didn't want to learn that the human mind is not a blank slate and is not by any means clean or innocent. On the contrary, Freud suggests, our subjective consciousness is only secondary, very incomplete, and all too often a profound falsification. We do not care for that, because we have been so Cartesian for so long. We have clung to our belief in the innocence of our religious experiences in the same way and for the same reasons as we have clung to our Cartesian notion of clear private consciousness, and to our scientific empiricism.

We have believed in individual consciousness as the inner space wherein real Truth is given to us and tested by us. We have felt confident that we can tell which of the psychic events cropping up in our souls has no natural cause and therefore must have been sent from Above. Freud or no Freud, these convictions have proved singularly durable.

They have, however, become overlaid by later developments. The two main superimposed strata might be called Methodist and Romantic. The Methodists linked puritanism with today's Evangelical, Pentecostal and Charismatic movements. The Romantics, and especially figures such as Wordsworth and Emerson, took religious experience out of the fellowship meeting and the chapel and made it natural. It became something like a mode of response to an unbounded whole of which one felt oneself to be a part, a response that was both intuitive and reconciling. Religious experience was aestheticised, but it remained in some sense informative, and people still see it as somehow warranting an optimistic view of life and the world.

This historical background, I submit, explains the way religious experience is handled in the work of modern apologists such as Sir Alistair Hardy and David Hay. In their surveys they have posed questions like: 'Have you ever been aware of or influenced by a presence or power, whether you call it God or not, which is different from your everyday self?' Alternatively: 'Have you ever felt as though you were very close to a powerful spiritual force that seemed to lift you out of yourself?' Over the past thirty years, in Britain and the USA, about a third of the population have been answering Yes to these questions (Hay, pp. 120–34), and I am arguing that the way the questions are framed and answered, and the way the answers are interpreted, is all to be explained against the historical background I have sketched. Our religious experiences are the product of our own particular cultural and intellectual history. Figures like Calvin and Descartes, Jonathan Edwards and John Wesley, Wordsworth and William James, gave us philosophical assumptions to which we still cling, instructed us that religious experiences were desirable, and prescribed the form that they must take—and, indeed, do take. Among us, at least. If we were Tibetans, our assumptions would be very different. But here and with this history behind us, we see things as we do, and take our way of seeing them for granted.

I hope I have now explained a paradox. People in our tradition assume that their own religious experiences are *not* historically conditioned, but are clean natural data given to them from Above. I have outlined an historical explanation of why they are systematically unaware of the historicality of their own religious experiences.

I don't mean to sound sceptical. I am no sceptic. But I am saying that historicising religious experience is the only way to make it intelligible. How else could we hope to explain the fact that every religious-experience report is as much tied to a particular cultural context as any other kind of writing? People's religious experiences invariably reflect locally-held beliefs. As Hume said in connection with miracles, the religious experiences of different religions would all cancel each other out, unless we can learn to see each religion as producing its own tradition of experience internally. Your religious experience is an *expression* of your local religious tradition, and not a piece of independent evidence for its truth.

The local religious background also makes the logic of religious experience intelligible. After all, the David Hay questions are very perplexing in terms of classical Christianity, which regarded God as unknowable. From patristic times God was infinite and simple, altogether transcending the categories through which the human mind might understand him. Nowadays, though, pollsters and respondents appear to share the assumption that some sort of knowledge-by-experience of God is possible. They even seem to suppose that there is a valid inference from 'I am in a certain psychological state', to 'I am experiencing none other than *God*'. How is this possible? The history I have sketched gives the answer. The puritans fully accepted that

God cannot be known directly, but in their theology the scripture-guided believer was justified in referring certain special states of the soul to God as their cause. This means that in their own way the puritans also set religious experience within an interpretative context. It is not clean or natural. It arises within a specific faith-community. Scripture forms it, and helps us to interpret it.

I'm saying something rather similar. The student of religion must explain religious experience purely immanently, that is, historically. Your religious experience is your religious and cultural tradition expressing itself through you and in your life-experience. Catholics have Catholic experiences, Protestants have Protestant experiences. Even within the Hebrew Bible it is already being said that the criterion of authenticity for a prophecy or vision is its conformity with the orthodox tradition that produced it and that it must reflect and confirm (e.g. Deuteronomy 13:1, 18:15–20). My culturalism or expressivism explains why conformity with the local orthodoxy has to be the criterion of genuineness. There cannot *be* any other criterion.

Very well. But suppose you accept all this: suppose you join me in seeking to become a fully-demythologised believer of the new post-realist kind. Can people like us still enjoy the consolations of religious experience? Yes, we can. It is true that we have given up the illusions of supernaturalism, and therefore have lost that sudden, compelling, given-from-outside quality. Our religion has become a continuous and fully immanent movement of signs. There is still innovation, but we know nothing of any violent irruption from outside. The world of signs is outsideless. Nevertheless, our religion can still be aesthetically beautiful, creative and joyous. After Truth, our religious experience coincides with our religious *activity*.

9

GOD BEYOND OBJECTIVITY (1991)

At home we used to have an old biscuit tin filled with miscellaneous pieces of the children's constructional toy, Lego, and there was a game of trying to build something recognizable that would use up as many of the pieces as possible. They couldn't all be used, for there were too many oddments, and they could of course be assembled into a variety of different shapes. Nevertheless, some solutions to the problem were manifestly better than others.

So it is with belief in God. We have inherited and we still use an extraordinary miscellany of idioms, ways of thinking and speaking about God. Nothing guarantees in advance that they will all fit together into one tidy systematic construction. Quite the opposite, for what we have is a jumble of fragments from kits acquired at different times in the past. Many pieces have been lost, and of those that survive some are more useful than others. No single logical thread ties them all together. We have to try to make what we can out of them; but we must remember that the more pieces we incorporate the more ragged and unstable will be the thing we construct, so it may be better to leave a good deal of material unused in the interests of building something stronger, more coherent and recognizable. That any rate is my own preference.

One further application of the analogy: people used to think that the Church or the Bible gave them a ready-made construction, or at least a complete kit of pieces designed to be assembled into just one construction. Today, though, our new sense of history and our closer study of the individual pieces has shown us that the Bible and the Christian tradition present us with something much more like my children's Lego tin, which grew slowly over many years with some substantial additions, and also many small losses that went unnoticed until we started building.

Most users of the Lego tin were quite happy to speak of 'the Lego' as if it were a unity, and had many hours of fun using the pieces as they came to hand to make what they pleased of them. A theologian is rather like a heavy parent who moves in with big systematic ambitions, and then starts complaining that the material is too incomplete for his design to be executed. He spoils the fun, but there it is. There are such people, and I am one of them. At least by now I have learnt to attempt something small. Like this:

When the heathens asked, 'Where is their God?', they were taunting a people in trouble. In the ancient world being a god was all about power, and nothing could be more galling than to be told that you were in such poor shape that your god was obviously absent or impotent. The heathen regarded a god as being a kind of tribal mascot or guardian angel. He embodied the people's identity and their cultural values, and he was supposed to look after them. In fact the god's prestige or glory rose and fell with his people's: when they were well-nourished he was evidently powerful and active on their behalf, but when things were going badly for them it seemed that he must be feeble or negligent. The internationally recognized glory of your god was in those days what the strength of your currency on the foreign-exchange markets is nowadays. National gods rose or fell and were strong or weak according to the prevailing perception of a nation's stability, vigour and prospects, much as today when the dollar is high Americans walk tall, the Churches flourish and the Administration does well in the polls; whereas when the dollar tumbles and people ask maliciously, 'Where is it now?', Americans feel humiliated. So in the Old Testament we often find great concern being expressed about God's international standing. He promises to make his name great among the nations by exalting Israel, for the glory of the god was indeed the chief index of national well-being, just as the strength of the currency is today. Hence the huge effort that went into building great temples and maintaining the cult.

However, although such ways of thinking about God and the function of religion are indeed found in the Old Testament, the Psalmist does not accept them. Staying within the same field of picture-language, he insists that the power and authority of the God of Israel does not decline like the currency when the nation's fortunes decline. As he puts it, God is not just a tribal mascot or an index of national prosperity, for 'he is in heaven and does whatever he wills'. God's sovereignty is absolute and logically independent of how Israel happens at the moment to be faring. Israel's strength may be variable, but God's is not.

How are we to interpret this affirmation? It seems that the faith of Israel is and has to be doggedly and deliberately counter-factual. You cannot infer what God is like from the way things go, because what is true of God is true *a priori,* or independently of the facts. This means that when things are going badly for you, you should not conclude that God has become weak or indifferent, for to make such an inference would be to relapse into the typically heathen notion of god. Admittedly, in bad times human faith may fail, but the failure in that case is a failure of human faith and not a failure of God. Like some other biblical writers, the Psalmist seems to be saying that God functions as a transcendent, supra-factual, *a priori* and necessary reference-point in human life, whose authority is not conditional upon the facts about how things are going, but is unchangeable.

We see this insight emerging in those biblical prayers in which people are wrestling with God and questioning his justice. As they work their way through their own violently conflicting feelings about God they gradually come to see that they are resolving a problem in their own religious psychology, rather than a problem in theology. Their prayer-struggle is resolved when they are at last able to grasp what is meant by the unchangeability of God. He is not an anthropomorphic tutelary deity, a personal protector whose job it is to protect us from harm. On the contrary, he is tough. He changes us the hard way, by being himself unchangeable. So the prayer of one who strives with God ends when he can at last bring himself to say, 'Nevertheless, not my will but thine be done. Amen'—and *that* is the victory of God. For the true God is victorious only when we have purged ourselves of the last remnants of the heathen conception of god.

All this makes clear the meaning of the most important and intense kind of prayer, the trial of faith in the time of affliction. It teaches the believer that God is not like the gods of the heathen. The true God is supernatural and not merely natural. He is a pure guiding spiritual ideal which constrains us. Being truly transcendent, he is not a fact and does not vary with the facts. His authority and power to save reside in his very eternity, immutability and invulnerability, for they mean that however bad things become he remains our refuge in just the same way. He is that which we should cling to whatever happens, because it remains reliable whatever happens.

God is therefore not a personal god in the same sense as the gods of the heathen are personal gods. What made the God of Israel Israel's god and bound them to him was not any special personal pay-off or protection that they could expect to receive, as if a Church were a Mafia family run by an exceptionally efficient Godfather. Rather, Israel was astonished to find that to her alone among ancient peoples had it been given to arrive at this peculiarly exalted, spiritual and consciousness-raising conception of God. Israel, it seemed, possessed the only god who was not his people's possession, because he was truly transcendent. Their tribal god was the only God who is *not* a tribal god. I am attempting to grasp what really is distinctive and out of the ordinary in the ancient Hebraic idea of God. I do not deny that my account uses only a small selection of the pieces available to us, and I admit that it is difficult and paradoxical, hard to get hold of and hard to retain. Nevertheless, I think it is what matters most. On it hinges the entire history of belief in God to this day, for the struggle between the heathen and the Israelite conceptions of God goes on perennially within Israel itself and within every one of us who believes in God, of whatever tradition. To be seriously committed to belief in God is to find yourself undergoing a progressive purging. Gradually the cosy objective personal god of the heathen is expelled and replaced by the more spiritual and demanding concept.

The shift is oddly difficult to describe. We can try various vocabularies, and talk about moving from heteronomous to autonomous faith, from a realist to a non-realist conception of God, from a natural to a truly super-natural God, from a metaphysical to an existential faith, from an external God to a God within, from objectivism to voluntarism, and so on. I have tried all these models, and others as well. They are all doubtless unsatisfactory. Never mind: the fact remains that belief in God allows you no rest. There is not any one true dogmatic philosophy of religion, as many people suppose, but instead only a long process of refinement or purification.

I am not talking about the conflict between universal and particularist or sectarian strands in belief. Some people have seen in the Bible a gradual movement from tribal to universal faith. The idea is that God starts like an old-style king, contracted to his people. He unifies them and has absolute sovereignty over them. He leads them in battle, and is glorified when they win and temporarily eclipsed when they lose. He is the fount of their law, and they petition him and are judged by him. Gradually in the Bible, though, this primitive idea is generalized and extended to the whole human race. God comes to be seen as the King of Kings and Lord of all the earth. All peoples stand in the same relation to him, and morality becomes universal—but, as we know too well, universal monotheists go on claiming that their own particular community nevertheless retains a special relationship with God. All the nations worship God, each in its own way, but *we* worship him in *his*.

Certainly there is a conflict of this type between universalism and sectarianism in the teachings of many religions, but it is not what I am here discussing. The deeper conflict is that between the heathens who see their god as being somehow factual and varying with the facts, and the Israelites whose God is supernatural. Call him a transcendent and unvarying reference-point for assessing human life whose potency lies precisely in the fact that he is not part of this changing world, and does not change; call him a pure guiding spiritual ideal; or cut out the personal pronouns altogether and speak only of a religious imperative: whatever your preference, it is hard to find the right words for the true God who is not an objective being, not a person, and does not exist as things exist. The great teachers speak of him as indescribable and incomprehensible, and say that since God cannot be talked about directly we must resort to indirect techniques. These techniques may include imaginative stories designed to break people out of their ordinary ways of thinking, expositions of the spiritual life to show how faith in God works practically, and even all-out iconoclastic attacks on the false heathen idea of god. They may all be used, but if they are used well they will hurt and will provoke anger, for true faith in God is what most people think of as atheism. So it always has been, and no doubt always will be.

Yet the clues are there. For God traditionally has two sets of attributes, the metaphysical and the moral. The metaphysical attributes decisively separate him from the world of fact, insisting that he is not in space or time and has no limits, body, parts or feelings. In short, he is like a pure ideal; and his moral attributes also remove him from the world of fact. Thus he is love, period. Not any particular love, neither an object-selecting love nor a selectable love-object, but love simple, universal and objectless—and therefore not himself an object. Indeed, the Christian ideal of love as universal, disinterested and selfless rules out the notion that God can be an objective personal being, because he cannot be thought of as one who is singled out from others as the preferred love-object, nor as one who himself singles out preferred objects of his love. So the ideal of love requires the decentring of God; and so also it is with God's other attributes of justice, wisdom, beauty, goodness and the rest.

It is this decentring both of God and of oneself in religion that makes the phrase 'my God' so paradoxical. To attain a kind of life-love which is subjectless and objectless and no longer egoistically or moralistically selective, I must become decentred and me and myness must go. I have to lose my possessions, my relationships, my very life and become nothing suspended in nothingness. I am only fit to use the word 'my' in connection with my God when . . . Nothing is mine. So, a final linguistic tease: God is such that when nothing is mine and I am nothing, then God is mine.

Part Three

Jesus Christ and Humanism

10

ONE JESUS, MANY CHRISTS? (1972)

Among men of religion the prophet Mohammed is one of the most clearly remembered. He was a man who, after considerable spiritual struggles, emerged as a passionate and eloquent prophet of the one God in his middle age. He had great practical gifts as warrior, organizer and statesman, but above all he was a man of God. We have this fairly distinct picture of Mohammed even though the first biography of him, by Ibn Ishaq, was not written till over a century after the prophet's death, and the various biographical traditions about him obviously stand in need of critical sifting. We have this distinct idea of Mohammed, even though the details of his biography are not central to the faith of Islam, but belong to the secondary material, the *hadith*. Through thirteen centuries Islam has been remarkably constant, and has always 'projected' a pretty constant picture of Mohammed. Critical sifting of the biographical traditions about him has not radically changed this picture, and there is considerable agreement about Mohammed among scholars. Perhaps it is just because it has never wished to worship him that Islam has never had any very strong interest in idealizing its picture of Mohammed.

The situation with Gautama, the Buddha, is rather different. The canon of sacred writings is very large and rather late. The tendency to make the Buddha himself the object of worship, or at least an instrument of contemplation, has distorted the picture of him. For example, it magnified his birth, changing his father from a minor chieftain into a great king: and in the familiar iconography his beatific expression bears no trace of the struggles of the historical man. Piety has idealized the Buddha; but nevertheless it can be said of him too that we have a fair idea of the kind of man he was, and of the issues which concerned him. He asked, what is man? What are the causes of suffering, and how can it be escaped? What is the final good for a human being, and how can it be attained? We know fairly well what answers he gave, and Buddhism too, in spite of the idealization, has projected a fairly constant image of the Buddha.

With Jesus the position is much less clear. He has been more intensely and directly worshipped by more different kinds of people than any other man, and this worship has blurred him. As we can faintly distinguish the historical Buddha beneath the smiling benignant Buddha of piety, so Christians have distinguished the Jesus of history from the divine Saviour of the developed ecclesiastical faith. But the truth is much more complex. Buddhist iconography projects one dominant image of the Buddha, but

Christian iconography has projected a great number of images of Jesus: there was the shepherd-teacher of the first few centuries; the *Christos pantocrator* of the period dominated by Byzantium; the twisted, naked crucified man of the later Christendom period; and there have been many others. From the very first the 'theologizing' of Jesus began to erase his human features, so that even though substantial, early and detailed books about him (which have the form of biographies) are at the centre of the canon of sacred writings, the figure of Jesus himself has remained enigmatic and capable of very diverse interpretations. He has been seen as moralist, prophet, apocalyptist, hero, redeemer, priest and king. People of the highest ability who have read the gospels afresh very closely have reached conclusions about Jesus much more varied than we could find in the case of Gautama or Mohammed.

The fact of varied interpretations of Jesus is notorious, and it has been said that everyone who writes a life of Jesus sees his own face at the bottom of a deep well. This is too simple, for while there is undoubtedly distortion, it is of more than one kind. We should first distinguish *positive* from *negative* distortion. Positive distortion occurs when the reader projects upon Jesus an ideal self-image. George Bernard Shaw, in his Preface to *Androcles and the Lion* (1915) described Jesus as a 'highly-civilized, cultivated person', a Bohemian socialist. William Blake, in *The Everlasting Gospel* (1818) portrayed Jesus as proud, independent and mocking. Tolstoy, in his later writings, saw Jesus as the same relentless moralist of altruistic love that he was himself. These are examples of positive distortion: negative distortion occurs when the reader discerns in Jesus all the qualities which he repudiates. Thus Nietzsche, in *The Antichrist* (written about 1888; published 1895) saw Jesus as something between an immature adolescent and a hypersensitive psychopath—Dostoyevsky's Idiot. The poet A. C. Swinburne in his *Hymn to Proserpine* (from *Poems and Ballads,* 1866) sees Jesus as a morbid ascetic who immolated himself before a cruel dying Father-God. Both in a way projected upon Jesus their own traits: Nietzsche was inclined to be a solitary valetudinarian, and Swinburne had sado-masochistic inclinations, if one may be forgiven the vulgarity of so categorizing them. But the point is that if they projected upon Jesus traits which were present in themselves, it was not as ideals to be pursued but as vices to be spurned.

A second distinction, cutting across the first, must also be made between two other kinds of distortion. Some writers, like Seeley and Renan, *assimilate* Jesus to the spirit of their own time, making him exemplify and authenticate the ideals current in their own society. Other writers, of whom Kierkegaard and Schweitzer are examples, emphasize the strangeness of Jesus, and make of him a stick with which to beat their contemporaries. They see Jesus as a *corrective* to the spirit of their own time, emphasizing that he lived by values unknown or abhorrent to most people nowadays. Schweitzer attacked some of his predecessors for positive distortion very effectively and has had great influence. His own corrective distortion is perhaps associated with his decision to go to Africa. At any rate, he and such later writers as Rudolf Bultmann and R. H. Lightfoot have tended to disseminate the opinion that the truest account of Jesus is one which says that he was an eschatological prophet, that we do not know a great deal about him, and that what little we do know is very strange to our ears. A rough generalization has gained currency to the effect that nineteenth-century pictures of Jesus were assimilatory and suffered from positive distortion, whereas twentieth-century pictures of Jesus are corrective and much more soundly based on scholarly study of the texts. I have already given sufficient reasons for thinking that that generalization is too crude and question-begging. It would be nearer the mark to say that in nineteenth-century religious controversy all four kinds of distortion are richly in evidence; whereas in the present century, a time when Christianity has been on the defensive and whose history has been ugly, corrective distortion has been more popular in theological circles. But positive distortions can still be found, as when Jesus is portrayed as a revolutionary nationalist leader.

Again, as we may contrast the historical Buddha with the Buddha of piety, so we may contrast Jesus with the Christ of later Christian piety. But since the French Revolution the climate of opinion has tended to be critical, humanist, anti-authoritarian and anti-ecclesiastical; so that the contrast between Jesus and the ecclesiastical Christ has generally been made to the latter's disadvantage. It is said that the Christ of Christian iconography—whether as represented in pictures or in theological formulae—is abstract, inhuman and antipathetic. A good and unfamiliar example of this complaint is to be found in H. G. Wells' *First and Last Things*.[1]

In reaction, many theologians (including Kähler, Tillich, Bousset, Bultmann and Barth) have nevertheless asserted that the Christ of Christianity, the preached and worshipped Christ, is the 'real' Christ and that the historical Jesus is a figure of no particular religious interest. The difficulty with this is that there is no single preached Christ. More recently there has been a swing back, and efforts have been made to define the relation between Jesus the eschatological prophet and the Christ of the early Christian preaching.

All this is an oft-told tale. My purpose in recalling it is simply to point out a paradox. More than any other religion Christianity has revolved obsessively around one particular man: it has loved him, worshipped him, meditated upon him, portrayed him, and sought to imitate him—but he slips away. Recently I heard someone essay the generalization that Islam is a religion of victory whereas Christianity's central imagery is of suffering and defeat. Yet the crucifixion of Jesus has not always and everywhere been seen as of central importance and even where the cross *has* been prominent it has been seen in many different ways. In the Anglo-Saxon poem *The Dream of the Rood* Jesus crucified is seen as an enthroned prince, and as a hero in battle: he is utterly different from the tortured, hideous figure of Grünewald's altarpiece at Isenheim. It is true that for much of its history Christianity has been a religion of salvation from sin, especially in the West, and Jesus has been seen as the divine redeemer who procures for us the forgiveness of sins. But this has not always been so, and especially in recent times there has been a marked swing away from the ideas of God the almighty and reproachful Father, the guilty sinner, and Jesus as mediator. There is at present more emphasis on Jesus as the pioneer of faith.

This great diversity of Christianity is partly the result of its having flourished in so many different cultures. At least five may be distinguished. There was Jewish Christianity; the Christianity of the ancient churches of countries like Syria, Ethiopia and South India; Eastern Orthodoxy, which grew out of Hellenistic culture; Latin or Roman Christianity; and the Protestantism of northern Europe. Within the remains of these older forms there perhaps exists in germ a sixth and new form of Christianity adapted to the global scientific culture which has been emerging in the last three centuries. Only Buddhism has found expression in a comparable variety of cultures.

But the image of Jesus is perplexingly vague and blurred. It is not surprising that theologians have wanted (rightly or wrongly) to clarify and stabilize it. They have had little success, and their close study of the New Testament has only made matters worse. For by now the critics distinguish several different accounts of Jesus which can be discerned within the New Testament itself. Here are some of them, in broad outline:

Jesus himself was—and saw himself as—an eschatological prophet who proclaimed the imminent coming of the Kingdom or God. He did not make 'claims' for himself: he did not claim divinity, he did not claim to be the Christ, and he did not even call *himself* the Son of Man. But he did regard his own work as helping to usher in the Kingdom of God, and, whatever was to happen to him, he hoped to be vindicated by the Son of Man at the end of time.

The second interpretation of Jesus is that of the earliest Palestinian Christianity. It began with the baptism of the man Jesus, and described his ministry as a prophet and servant of God. After his death he was, in his followers' eyes, vindicated by God. He now waits in heaven, and his followers gather a band who wait on earth for the time when he shall return as *himself* the Christ, the glorious Son of Man. When he comes thus, the present historical 'world' or 'age' will end.

The third interpretation of Jesus developed among the Greek-speaking Jews of the diaspora. Jesus is thought of as sent by God to be, during his life on earth, Son of David, Lord and Christ. At his exaltation he begins a period of heavenly reign over his church below which will culminate in the *parousia.*

The fourth interpretation of Jesus was that which appeared in the Greek world. The Gentile world longed for deliverance from sin, suffering and death. It was told of a pre-existent one. God's Word or Son, who descended to earth, became incarnate, defeated the demonic powers in a titanic struggle which ended his earthly life, returned in glory to his proper home in heaven, and now heads a new order of humanity which will be consummated in him.

Here, then, set out in a rather schematic way, are four very different accounts of Jesus to be found in the New Testament, which itself arose from the interaction of different cultures. Since the New Testament itself exhibits the translation of Christianity from one culture to another it is surprising that so many Christians are sceptical about whether Christianity can be so translated in our own time. And the development did not stop there, but has continued ever since, as Jesus has been ever more elaborately mythicized, demythicized and remythicized. Though the Christian tradition has almost constantly affirmed the reality of Jesus' manhood, it has with equal regularity idealized away, recovered, and then idealized away again his human characteristics, rather as in eastern Europe icons are effaced by pious kisses, repainted, and effaced again.

As there has been a long line of books attempting to isolate and define 'the essence of Christianity', so a great deal of ink has been spilt in endeavouring to give Jesus a clearer and more determinate outline. Indeed the 'quest of the historical Jesus' was undertaken in the hope of finding in him the essence of Christianity. Jesus is an example of the ancient philosophical problem of identity and change: it is hoped to distinguish the substance of what he is from the accidental dress in which various ages have clothed him. Surely if Christianity is one religion and not many religions, it ought to be possible to say something about the one Christ in whom all Christians have in their different ways believed? Tradition has counted for a great deal in Christianity, and Christians have generally wished to affirm that they believe in the same Christ as St Paul believed in, and believe in him in the same way.

But Christians have been exceedingly diverse. An immense variety of ideals of character have been ostensibly based upon the example of Jesus: an historical man who lived only one life has been made the exemplar of a great range of different forms of life. Jesus has been declared to be a model for hermits, peasants, gentlemen, revolutionaries, pacifists, feudal lords, soldiers and others. Even if we restricted attention to the religious life of men in the Latin West alone, the diversity is great among the ideals of Benedict, Francis, Bruno and Ignatius Loyola.

One solution has been to recognize this diversity and generalize the notion of Christ. That is to say, the term 'Christ' is understood to denote an abstract principle of moral perfection, or of harmony with the divine, of which Jesus is one concrete and perfect instance but which may become concrete in other lives in a variety of different ways. Thus there may be a rough 'family resemblance' among all the actual Christ-lives which justifies us in predicating 'Christhood' of them all, but they need not all closely resemble the life of Jesus himself. The traditional doctrine was that there is and can be only one Christ, namely Jesus, *in the same way* that there is and can be only one divine being, namely, God. So just as 'God' is both a predicable term and the proper name of an individual, so Christ is both a predicable term and the proper name of an individual. The result is that there is only one concrete way of being Christ-like, namely Jesus' own way. But this traditional and very 'strong' doctrine of the unity of Christ fails to explain the extraordinary variety of the Christian tradition. The historian notices how differently Jesus has been seen at different times and places, and what a variety of life-styles have been ostensibly based on his example: and the theologian must ask himself how the individual characteristics of the historical Jesus can be reconciled with the host of life-styles which he has been called upon to validate and exemplify.

Thus there has been a strong inclination to detach Christ from Jesus, or at any rate to change the logical knots by which Jesus and Christ have hitherto been tied together to make the complex entity 'Jesus Christ'.

A striking example can be quoted from Florence Nightingale. In her book *The Cause* (1929), Ray Strachey printed an extract from an unpublished confessional work by Miss Nightingale on 'the Woman Question'. She writes about the theological problem created for her by the extraordinary disabilities of women in the 1850s, and she sees herself as 'Cassandra', the prophetess of 'a female Christ, who will resume in her own soul the sufferings of her race'. Florence Nightingale was a Christian, but the position of women in her time was such that the full humanity of women was denied by society with, it seemed, the approval of the church. Jesus was a man and in Florence Nightingale's day hardly a man alive could understand what women were aggrieved about. The intellectual stress she suffered separated 'Jesus' from 'Christ' in her mind, and she became one of the first Christians to formulate the remarkably original idea of a female Christ.

Another way in which Christ could be detached from Jesus was through reflection on the limitations of our historical knowledge of Jesus. For Kant the idea of Christ was *a priori*: the term 'Christ' denotes the idea of moral perfection realized in a human being. We may find reason to judge that Jesus instantiated this concept historically; but such an historical Judgment can never be more than probable, whereas we know with certainty what is really important to us, namely that moral perfection can be and must be realized in our lives. Thus for Kant the moral force of the Christ-idea is independent of any claim that it has been embodied historically in Jesus. When the possibility that Jesus had never lived was put to Tolstoy he said the same.[2]

For Hegel the term 'Christ' signifies the ideal union of human and divine spirits—a goal to which the entire historical process moves. The connection between Jesus and Christ is contingent, and certainly not exclusive.

So it would seem to be possible for people to experience a *religious* longing for a Christ, and the moral power of the Christ-idea, apart from any specific and exclusive claim that any actual man, such as Jesus, is the one and only Christ. One of the best examples is the Sufi doctrine of the Perfect Man. The Perfect Man somewhat resembles the idealized Adam of the rabbis, or the Heavenly Man of some ancient gnostics. He was the self-revelation of God, his visible image: he could be called the final cause of the universe, and the expression of God's will to be known. He could be seen as embodied in the Prophet, or the saints of Islam: he could also be seen in woman. R. A. Nicholson states that 'Ibnu'l-'Arabï went so far as to say that the most perfect vision of God is enjoyed by those who contemplate him in woman; and Rumï speaks in a similar vein.[3] The Perfect Man is in fact a schema—the notion of a human being perfectly responsive to God and so a revelation of him—a schema which different believers may apply and use in different ways. Its religious value and efficacy is not thought to depend on the claim that it has been embodied once for all in one particular person.

Our argument so far suggests a reason for the vagueness of Jesus. In the Christian phenomenon as a whole, 'Christ' has meant so many different things, and being Christ-like has meant so many very different ways of life, that talk of Christ must either break away from any exclusive association with Jesus of Nazareth or be severely pruned back. The first alternative was chosen by the idealists, who made of Christ the general principle or pattern of relationship between the human spirit and the divine: a pattern which maybe was exemplified in Jesus but which may equally be exemplified in any number of other men. The second alternative was to try to fix the historical Jesus and use him to cut back the luxuriant growth of ecclesiastical Christianity. Christianity would be reconstructed on the basis of the Jesus of history, and in the process drastically simplified and clarified. The range of possible ways **of** being Christ-like and talking of Christ would be narrowed sufficiently for Jesus to be able to hold them together.

A liberal Christian who is told that the quest for the Jesus of history has failed finds himself wondering where he shall find his starting point. What is Christianity for him? Critics of Christianity sometimes try to play fair by defining at the outset what it is they propose to attack. And they discover that whatever they say Christianity is, someone will dispute the definition. The liberal Christian is in the same difficulty if he tries to say who Jesus Christ is, and what he means by the unity of Christ and by the finality of Christ.

We do not escape the difficulty if we turn to consider, not the historical Jesus himself, but the doctrinal propositions about him which have long been thought to constitute the *differentia* of Christianity. Four of these might be that Jesus was born of a virgin, that he was and is both divine and human (or that he is the Son of God), that by his death the forgiveness of our sins has been procured, and that he rose from the dead. Each of these propositions seems at first sight tolerably clear and definite (whether it be thought true or false): but as soon as we begin the study of the history of Christian theology it becomes apparent that none of them is anything of the kind. There is no such thing as an orthodox christology, even though for purposes of church government it has often been claimed that there is. There is not even any such thing as a New Testament doctrine about Christ. As soon as you try to state it you are at once obliged to admit that your statement is interpreted rather differently by different New Testament writers. I doubt if you could write down *any* statement about Christ to which St Mark, St Paul, St John and the writer to the Hebrews would demonstrably have assented in precisely the same sense.

For example, the early Christians certainly held that Jesus was risen, but exactly what they meant by this is a matter of considerable and even acrimonious controversy. Did they mean that his corpse had revived in the grave, walked out of it again, and thereafter been physically seen by his disciples? Did they mean that at their meetings to break bread they had enjoyed visions of him while in a state of ecstasy? Did they mean that they had pored over the Old Testament and were now announcing, in the prophetic manner, that the God of Israel had approved the work and exalted the person of his servant Jesus? Did they mean that a divine man had descended from heaven, sojourned awhile on earth, and was now returned to his proper home? I have elsewhere argued for one of these opinions,[4] but I am bound to admit that some early Christians may have held one, and some another. I cannot assume that they all held the same opinion, when they manifestly speak about the resurrection in different ways.

Thus the diversity of Christianity is such that it is hard to see how a clear agreed picture of Jesus himself, or an agreed list of basic christological assertions, could be settled upon. One is bound to ask, how strong *is* Christian interest in the unity of Christ?

In the West people are used to the idea of visibly distinct religious communities. Christians sing 'One Church, one Faith, one Lord', and Judaism and Islam too have historically been hard-edged communities. A man was in no doubt to which he belonged. Westerners find Hinduism hard to understand precisely because it lacks such clear frontiers. To understand Hinduism one might invoke the famous disagreement between Socrates and Wittgenstein about universal concepts. Socrates thought that the prerequisite for rational enquiry in such fields as ethics was to establish clear and distinct universal concepts from which 'syllogizing' could begin. Wittgenstein, on the other hand, considered that the meanings of many important universal terms were not clear and distinct, and used the metaphor of a family resemblance among a class of individuals.

Similarly, our Western idea of the unity of a religion has in the past been Socratic, and the search for the essence of Christianity has been rather like Socrates' quest for exact definitions. But in Hinduism such a thing is plainly out of the question. What we find is rather a family resemblance among a large body of religious doctrines, cults, and movements.

Are we all moving in the direction of Hinduism? The religions used to be geographically distinguished in old atlases, but nowadays there are at least some adherents of most major religions in most countries. For centuries the influence of Jesus has by no means been confined to Christianity. For example, Tolstoy discerned in the gospels a repudiation of any exercise of coercive force. Gandhi picked it up from Tolstoy, and Martin Luther King picked it up from Gandhi. A religious idea twice moved across traditional religious frontiers within fifty years.

We may now tentatively suggest a few lines for further reflection. In the first place, as an historic organization Christianity, with its hierarchy and its discipline, had an almost military idea of its own unity. The slogan 'One Chuch, one Faith, one Lord' well epitomizes this, and in the ecumenical movement one can discern a nostalgia for that past ideal. Nevertheless it is in irreversible decline. Christianity is rather a family of monotheistic faiths which in various ways find in Jesus a key to the relation of man with God. It has and will continue to have almost as much internal diversity as Hinduism.

Both the unity and the diversity are important. It is important that the various forms of Christianity should maintain relations with the gospels, and that in each the Christ who is believed and preached today should interact with the Jesus who dimly emerges from the study of the New Testament. This common endeavour consolidates family ties.

But the study of the gospels has itself shown that Jesus' mission was not to draw attention to himself, or to promulgate doctrines about himself. He was a signpost, not a destination. He pointed men to God and told them about the claims of God and the nearness of God. His own career exhibited what it is to believe in God. To be a Christian is in one's own way to be stimulated by him to become engaged with the reality of God. It was always a mistake to make Jesus himself the direct object of worship. A good many forms of Christianity appear at first glance to fall into this error, and Jews and Moslems have rightly protested against it, as being incompatible with monotheism. But on closer examination one notices, for example, that in the historic Christian liturgies prayer was and is addressed *to* God *through* Christ. Official forms of prayer directly addressed to Christ or to the Holy Spirit are always uncommon, and for the most part late. Christianity has for the most part been a form of monotheism guided by Jesus seen as Christ, and if this were more generally understood relations between Christians and members of so-called 'other faiths' would be easier.

So I suggest that the problem of the one and the many in the Christian tradition—and particularly in the figure of Christ—is becoming a little easier. Modern study of the gospels tells against the opinion that the purpose of Jesus was to create a highly-unified cultus of himself as the divine Christ, a cultus definable in dogmatic formulae, and maintained by a sharply-defined church community. Jesus' legacy to mankind is rather an urgent appeal to each of us to acknowledge above all else the reality of God. I call him Christ insofar as I respond to this summons and find in the gospels the pattern or shape of what it is to obey it. But the way he is Christ for me may be very different from the way he is Christ for some other person, and (if I may speak crudely) he himself is not troubled by being many Christs, or Christ in many ways. Nor is he in the least concerned about the disintegration of the 'One Church, one Faith, one Lord' ideal. It was not followers in the Way who themselves invented the term 'Christian', and it is arguable that it is *almost* as serious a misnomer as 'Mohammedan' or 'Wesleyan'.

So I agree with the liberals that, in a rather loose way, allegiance to the historical Jesus holds together the various forms of Christianity. But we do not know enough of him to use him to prune back the variety of styles of faith and life which have stemmed from him. So I agree with the modernists in valuing that variety. Jesus' mission was not to create a cultus of himself as divine Christ, but to point away from himself to God. Hence his elusiveness, symbolized by St Mark in the so-called 'messianic secret'. God can be believed in and served in as many ways as there are people. In the Christian tradition Jesus is the paradigm of faith, but that paradigm may be re-enacted in a great variety of ways, and we need not labour to reduce their number.

11

ON THE FINALITY OF
CHRIST (1975)

Except in the Moslem world, and in the most populous parts of Asia, Christianity has become in modern times the principal religious faith of mankind. The revival and expansion of the Roman Catholic Church since the middle of the nineteenth century have been especially remarkable. The process of decolonization has not in any way reduced the power and attractiveness of European culture. Even China, although at present (1975) in one of its xenophobic phases, remains under the sway of a European political ideology, and European science and technology.

Yet there is a paradox in all this. For as European culture has become global, Europe itself has declined in power and confidence; as Roman Catholicism has nourished and spread under the inspiration of ultramontanism, it has come to experience a crisis of authority; and as the influence of Christ and the Christian movement have become world-wide, many Christians have come to doubt the absoluteness of Christianity and the finality of Christ. It has become conventional in the so-called 'Western' countries to deplore the cultural and the religious imperialism of our nineteenth-century forebears, while yet in many respects the triumphal progress of Western-style industrialization, of socialism, and of Christian expansion still continues. Christian doubts about the finality of Christ are surely part of the wider paradox of the European *daimon*. We colonized Africa, but we could not help sowing in it the political and moral ideas which would in time enable it to rise up and expel us. We went out as missionaries of Christ, but we also could not but encourage the peoples we encountered to rediscover and reaffirm their own ancient faiths against ours. Forced to concede moral and political parity in the one case, we are now increasingly inclined to accord them religious parity in the other.

It is against this background that we can best see how traditional Christianity developed its understanding of the finality of Christ, and why it has run into difficulties in modern times.

I

No reader of the New Testament can fail to observe that its most fundamental affirmation concerns the uniqueness, the sole sufficiency, and the finality of what God has done in Jesus Christ. This conviction is expressed in various ways, and it is not altogether easy to clarify and define it, but of its presence there can be no doubt. That Jesus is God's only Son; that only through him can humans be saved; that God acted in him once and for all; that world history will be wound up by him; and that he is God's chief executive, seated henceforth at God's right hand: these are some of the forms in which it is expressed. The events described in the Gospels are unique and unrepeatable. What is happening here is such as has never happened before, and can never happen again. It is quite compatible with Buddhism, indeed it is held by Buddhists, that the state of Enlightenment attained by the Buddha under the Bo-tree may be independently reached by other men before and since: whereas Christianity regards the life, death, and resurrection of Christ as in some way essentially unique and unrepeatable. But already we are in need of more precise statement, for surely Jesus himself said that the rejection, persecution, execution, and vindication of a righteous man is something that has all too often happened before, and will often happen again? The pattern of his ministry, suffering, death, and resurrection is, he declares, amply foreshadowed in old tradition and will be re-enacted, both in ritual and life, in the future. So what is unique about this particular enactment of the pattern? The answer seems to be that all the earlier enactments were anticipations of it, and all the later ones will take place in the power of it. That is to say, the special and unique status of the Christ-event is relative to a theology of history. For the Jews, like other peoples, divided time into great epochs, which were differentiated theologically. What makes Christ final is that he winds up one epoch and initiates a new one, whose character will be determined by him. Thus the idea of a change of dispensation, the end of an old order and the beginning of a new, is needed in order to explain the finality of Christ.

But we still do not have enough, for according to the Bible there had been such changes of dispensation before. One was marked by the eating of the forbidden fruit and man's expulsion from Paradise; another by the Flood and the Bow in the Cloud; another by Abram's leaving Ur and his arrival in Canaan; and another by the Exodus and the giving of the Law on Mount Sinai. If the age of Moses had been ended by Christ, why should not Christ in turn similarly give place to another? The answer, of course, is that the age Christ inaugurates is the Last Age. He cannot be superseded, for his age is necessarily final, and so he is final.

We notice here that if Christians seriously embrace the idea of a post-Christian era, they must on this account abandon the finality of Christ: and indeed must cease to be Christians in the sense normal hitherto.

So far then we have established that Christ's finality and absoluteness were explained by reference to an eschatological scheme, and a Jewish one at that. But if so, is not the message about Jesus strictly relative to Jewish religion and tradition? How can it be intelligible outside that context? In the earliest Church the decision to take the Gospel to the gentile world was reached only with difficulty. At any rate it was necessary, if you were to become a Christian, to accept the Jewish theology of history, and every Christian must become a kind of spiritual Jew before he could grasp the place of Christ in God's unfolding plan for mankind. The Hebrew Bible, or the Septuagint, must be canonized. To appreciate the finality of the New Dispensation you must first accept, and see yourself as having in some way been involved in, the Old.

Still more important, you must accept the Jews' own estimate of their own central place in universal history, as a light to the gentiles, the trunk of the human tree, and the people whose history is of universal significance.

Until as recently as the seventeenth century this worked remarkably well. The Bible is, after all, a very wide-ranging book. It knows Africa, Asia and Europe, and the civilizations of Mesopotamia, Egypt, Greece and Rome. It knows tribal, agricultural and urban society. Until the seventeenth century all Christian people, wherever they lived, saw universal history, and their own spiritual pedigree, as running back through Rome, Greece, Israel, Egypt, and on to Mesopotamia. Jews spread alongside Christians; and it is worth remembering, alongside the tragedy of that relationship, that the Jews were in a strange way necessary to Christians, as living monuments to the Christian view of the past. The Old Testament was the chief source-book for the early chapters of universal history, and there was no very significant conflict between the Christian understanding of the past and the best available secular evidence. In such a context the idea of the finality of Christ fitted surprisingly well. The basic distinction in world-history was that between A.D. and B.C. In the years before Christ people lived under the Law: those were the years of the slave-societies of remote antiquity. In the years of Grace men had come to mature freedom in Christ. Now the world was hastening to its end. For until the end of the seventeenth century time past and time future were both thought of as finite. Human history reached back to the beginning of the world, which indeed had been made for no other purpose than the acting-out of the drama of salvation. There had been about 4000 years before Christ, and there would be 1000 (as was at first thought) or perhaps 2000 years after him. Thus the drama was now in its last act; and we are reminded that not only was world history finite, but its whole course was seen as analogous to the course of a human life, and the Bible was a literary expression of the whole of it.

So the finality of Christ was understood at first in relation to Jewish eschatological ideas. When the Christian faith moved into the Greco-Roman world it successfully assimilated the culture it found. From Irenaeus to Milton the Christian world-view was a remarkably vigorous and successful elaboration of the Jewish sacred history, giving a comprehensive and impressively accurate historical-theological pedigree to all the known civilized world. The finality of Christ was preached in relation to this entire system.

And this is why we began with the paradox of Christianity's simultaneous expansion and loss of confidence. Since Milton's time the unity of Christian culture has been broken up by a huge enlargement of our perspectives in several dimensions at once. In the days of Leibniz and Newton the doctrine of progress appeared, with the denial of the finitude of future history, and so by implication of the finality of Christ. Even before then the voyages of exploration had made it plain that there were many human societies beyond the reach of any plausible extension of the usual historical-theological framework. What was the relation of the God of Christendom to Japan, or to the American peoples? Since Mark Twain jeered at it as 'chloroform in print', the Book of Mormon has been more laughed at than read. But it bravely sets out to answer an important question: What is the place of the New World in God's plan of salvation? It gives the New World a sacred pedigree parallel to the Old World's and cross-linked with it. Similar attempts are still being made on behalf of the Far East. If we think them absurd, then it is clear that we no longer believe that our religious and cultural pedigree is coextensive with the entire race, but rather recognize that it is only one of several such pedigrees.

A compromise has been suggested, among others by Dr Raymond Pannikar in *The Unknown Christ of Hinduism* (London, 1965), to the effect that since Christ is universal he finalizes not just one, but every great religious tradition. He is the fulfilment of the aspirations of India as much as of Israel. It is unrealistic and unnecessary to require Indians to renounce their own religious heritage and adopt the Hebrew Bible as their only way to Christ. In Europe the New Testament is prefixed by the Hebrew Bible. But in India it would surely be appropriate to preface the New Testament with Indian sacred books such as the Upanisads. To Christianize India is not to persuade her to disclaim her heritage, but rather to show Christ to her as its fulfilment.

One appreciates the cultural pressures which have given rise to this suggestion; pressures felt in a very acute form by Arab Christians in the Middle East today. But there are difficulties. How can the finality of Christ be proclaimed except in relation to the Jewish idea of history? Where time is cyclical there can be no *unrepeatable* incarnation: and unless God is orchestrating the historical process towards a climax there can be no place for a *final* incarnation. The doctrine of the finality of Christ is inescapably bound up with a view of time peculiar to the Jews, and so the New Testament cannot be separated from the Old.

The importance of the idea of time was realized in an amusing way by an obscure theologian called John Craig. He followed Locke in accepting the view that the credibility of testimony decays with the passage of time and so, in a book published in 1699, argued that the historical facts of Jesus' life must cease to be believed by the year A.D. 3150.[1] Craig concluded that Christ must return by then, but what is really striking about his argument is that, for the first time I think, a theologian has seen the problem of relating the finality of Christ to a possibly-indefinite futurity here on earth.

There have been other similar enlargements of perspective. As long ago as 1600 it was possible to speculate that the universe might contain other inhabited worlds than our own. Was the Christian revelation for them also, or did it relate to this world only?

Again, during the eighteenth century people were becoming accustomed to the idea that the world might be everlasting in past time, as well as in future time. The curtain may have been raised for countless ages before any human actors appeared. The word *aeon,* which in the Bible means a period of around 1,000 years, is now used by scientists to denote a period of one thousand million years.

So the idea that the Old Testament was the trunk of the tree of universal history was already in some difficulty in the eighteenth century, when a still more serious development took place, in the growing dissociation of theology from history. David Hume and others wrote history in a new detached spirit which seemed surprisingly free from any ideological or moral patterning. The new critical history began to demythologize the past, to deprive it of its power to shape a world-view and guide life, and so undermined not merely the Christian but any and every religious or mythical picture of the sacred past. Soon Lessing was to ask his famous question: How can necessary truths of reason be derived from contingent historical facts? If history contains nothing but finely judged probabilities, if everything in history is relative, then we can never justifiably claim to have discerned the absolute and the certain in history. There can never be historical evidence sufficient to prove that a man's death in Palestine is of eternal significance to me today. I may lean on Church history and say that the meaning of that man's death is so deeply a part of our cultural history that we must all come to terms with it. The psychologist C. G. Jung would have said that much. But such an argument does not even pretend to be applicable to a Buddhist monk in Sri Lanka.

II

So much, then, for the classical Christian way of explaining belief in the finality of Christ, by embedding it in a panoramic theology of history. One leading theologian of today, Wolfhart Pannenberg, has attempted to revive the idea of a Christian understanding of universal history. How successful he will be only time can tell, but the intellectual difficulties are by now formidable. What other possibilities are there?

The principal one, also rooted in the New Testament, explains the finality of Christ by relating it to a theological anthropology or (in a more modern idiom) an existential analysis of the human condition. The aim is to establish certain universal generalizations about all humans who ever have lived or will live. These statements are of somewhat uncertain status. They touch upon the fields of metaphysics, ethics, and psychology. Sometimes they seem to be necessary truths to which there can be no exceptions, and sometimes they seem to be empirical generalizations, confirmed or otherwise in our daily experience. Their status is something of a problem, but every culture and religion makes such statements, for there is always some implicit or explicit model of man; so let us not trouble ourselves further about their status, but simply recite them, as follows: Man is a rational creature, made by God and for God, the supreme end of whose existence is to know and enjoy God eternally. Now, to know God one must please him, and to please him one must be righteous and do the works of righteousness. But though man has some knowledge of what righteousness is—enough to know he lacks it—he lacks the power to do it. He is in the predicament known as the bondage of the will. He knows what is the road to lasting happiness, but cannot make any progress along it. His despair and need of a saviour are total: he needs one who can effect a total transformation of the self in him. For him, when he discovers Christ to be such a saviour, that saviour is final; for the saviour does nothing less than re-create him, rescuing him from utter damnation for eternal happiness.

The great Protestant anthropologies, from Luther to Ritschl, Bultmann, and Tillich, explain the finality of Christ in terms of the desperate predicament from which he rescues the believer, and the total re-creation of the self which he brings about. To enforce the point a whole series of extreme assertions is produced. Man prior to justification is wholly wicked, his will utterly in bondage, and he is therefore shut off from God and the hope of heaven. He can do nothing to save himself, for he is corrupt through and through. No non-Christian can be saved, or please God in any way at all.

The Protestant anthropology, and the psychological and moral outlook created by it, have been deeply influential but are now of course almost totally rejected by all modern people. And indeed it is open to very damaging criticisms. The extreme dualism implied in the doctrines of sin and redemption is not easy to reconcile with the universalism implied in the Christian doctrine of creation. There will be a suspicion that the diagnosis of the disease has been framed in such terms as to make it evident that only Christ can be the remedy. Indeed, this is true historically, for early Christianity consciously set up a complex parallel between Adam, the prototype of fallen man, and Christ, the prototype of redeemed man; and some theologians, such as Karl Barth, have in any case quite openly derived their account of man's disease from their account of God's remedy for it. What is more, how can the universality and objectivity of the Christian doctrine of fallen man be proved to people outside the Christian tradition, when the claims are no longer made that we are all descended from an original pair, that the Fall was an historical event, and that the effects of the Fall are transmitted to all their descendants? To humans outside the Christian tradition it will surely seem that the Protestant anthropology is not an absolute diagnosis of the universal human condition but a cultural product, intelligible in one cultural setting but irrelevant in another.

Doctrines are of course not only descriptive but prescriptive. They *recommend* a certain perspective. Perhaps the Protestant anthropology is not purporting to be an accurate analysis of how an Indian sees his own situation before God, but is rather a *recommendation* to adopt a certain self-understanding? In that case it must presumably be tested ethically: and so it becomes vulnerable to the severe moral criticisms that have so often been levelled against it, and which, to my mind, are conclusive.

III

The classical Christian account of the finality of Christ set it in the context of a great theological account of universal history. Christ was final because the Christian era was the Last Age of the world. The typical Protestant explanation of the finality of Christ grounded it upon the experience of redemption from a state of utter despair and damnation. The doctrine of man showed him to be trapped and lost without Christ, freed and saved in Christ.

We have found reason to be dissatisfied with both these accounts; but, in any case, it may well be retorted that we have so far begged the most important question of all. Christ is final, not just because of the part he is found to play in the drama of cosmic redemption, or individual redemption, but because of his own unique relation to God. For according to Christianity, Jesus Christ is the only-begotten Son of God, incarnate once for all in human form. It is not that Jesus' status depends upon the role he plays in the redemption drama, but that because he is God Incarnate the redemption drama unfolds around him. The fundamental idea is that there has been a unique embodiment of God in that short stretch of past history which was the life of Jesus. Starting from this conviction a theological picture of the world, or of the human heart, prior to his coming, and a theological picture at the new situation which the Incarnation creates, can both be constructed.

At any rate, the Incarnation is the fundamental idea, and it is in some degree independent of the two themes we have hitherto discussed: for one *could* hold that there has been an unrepeatable embodiment of God in Jesus of Nazareth, without being committed to any one particular apocalyptic or dispensational view of history, or any particular view of man fallen and redeemed. And if Jesus' status is thus independent, it can be reaffirmed outside its original apocalyptic context.

However, a belief in the Incarnation which is not set in *any* context is empty. Some reasons have to be given for believing it, and its religious implications have to be spelt out in some way. If the doctrine of the Incarnation be maintained in a very strong form, the case might be made somewhat as follows:

There has been a once-for-all inhistorization (to use H. H. Farmer's term[2]) of God in Jesus of Nazareth. This event is unique, and above reason. Given the modern understanding of the nature of historical knowledge, its occurrence admittedly cannot be proved by historical method alone. To take an obvious example, the sinlessness of Christ can scarcely be proved from the modest, and controversial, evidence we have for the life of Jesus. But the Incarnation is at least *consonant* with the recorded evidence as to Jesus' character, teaching, miracles, and resurrection, and the long tradition of Christian faith. All these strands of evidence point to a mystery which they cannot *compel* us, but may well *lead* us, to acknowledge.

Furthermore, if God has embodied himself absolutely in a particular life, then this event will leave a historical residue behind it. It will leave mementos. So a strong doctrine of the Incarnation, as many Catholic theologians have rightly claimed, becomes the base upon which a whole series of subsequent doctrines are piled: the physical resurrection of Christ, his real presence in the Eucharist, the infallibility of the Church which witnesses to him, and so on—the whole edifice, in fact, of feudal or 'Christendom' Christianity. An absolute incarnation of God in time means that there can be a visible absolute authority in matters of faith and morals. Here we have, I believe, the central theme of the neo-mediaeval and authoritarian forms of Christianity which flourished between the mid-nineteenth and mid-twentieth centuries, and which had a powerful appeal to people whose souls craved dogmatic certainty. It is the sudden failure of confidence in this kind of Christianity which has so unnerved people in recent years.

Yet there were obvious objections to this very positive and strong form of incarnation doctrine. Its demand for unconditional commitment and submission to authority has exposed it to increasing moral criticism, and given rise to a well-founded suspicion that its intellectual bases are not very strong. Its insistence that the man Jesus of Nazareth is an absolute image of

God in human form is not consistent, as Jews and Moslems are well aware, with classical monotheism. The eternal God and a historical man are two beings of quite different ontological status. It is simply unintelligible to declare them identical. What is more, the humanism of our age, which guides us in our reading of the Gospels, shows us in them a quite different figure from the Jesus of the high incarnationalists. According to the high incarnationalists, Jesus claimed to be God. Yet when we read the Gospels Jesus appears as one who prays to God, whose relation to God is one of faith, not identity, and who repeatedly denies that he in any sense 'is' God.[3] He suffers, he is tempted, he experiences storms of anger, exultant triumph, despair, compassion, and joy. He is not at all like a stately immobile icon of God. He does not appear as one who *embodies* God, but as one who with the whole of his passionate nature witnesses *to* God.

So the strong incarnationalist doctrine, that Jesus of Nazareth is an absolute icon of God, looks very implausible now. It developed at the moment when the old Christologies of Jesus as the Word of God, or as the Spirit-filled Man of God, were replaced by the new Christology of Jesus as God's only-begotten Son. And this happened just in time for Constantine. A father and his son are two beings of the same kind, and the son can indeed be a second edition, a replica of his father: whereas a man and his utterance are two things of *different* kinds. A Christology of Jesus as the Word of God is obviously, from a theological point of view, much less misleading than a Christology of Jesus as God's only son. But feudal Christianity needed a Son of God to validate the whole structure of society. A high incarnational Christianity says the things feudalism wants to hear; that man was created for serfdom, and that there is a historical absolute to which he must wholly submit himself. No doubt many Christians today will find all this offensive, but I fear it is uncomfortably close to the truth; and it explains why modern political upheavals, and above all the cry for liberation, have created a historical situation in which high incarnationalist Christianity cannot be defended successfully.

It is a strange and sad paradox, that the Protestant anthropology should in practice so often create an inner, psychological deformation and tyranny, and that the doctrine of the Incarnation should so readily lend itself to the establishment of an external and objective tyranny. Christ came to set men free, but modem man, who certainly longs for freedom, sees in the usual Christian accounts of Christ only forms and sources of enslavement. It is, perhaps, this realization that has set so many searching for a new kind of Christology, free from the moral ambiguities which have disfigured the older kinds. It is a reminder to us, in our present inquiry, of the dangers which beset any attempt to articulate the finality of Christ.

IV

So we turn at last to my constructive proposal, which seeks to steer a mid-course between the pure religious relativism which says that every major religion is an equally valid way to God, and the absolutist language in which traditional Christian faith has so often been expressed.

My argument is that we should think of Christ, not in terms of Son and Image, but in such terms as *Word* and *Witness*. Theology says there cannot be any wholly adequate temporal image of the eternal and invisible God, and history says that nothing historical can be absolute and certain. Morality says that an absolute historical incarnation of God must generate a reactionary and tyrannical social order. So for me, Jesus' finality lies not in himself but (as he himself says) in what he proclaims, and in the way he bears witness to it. Jesus is final, not as an absolute icon of God—there cannot be such a thing—but because of the way he bears witness to what is final and unsurpassable. His finality is relative to man's spiritual aspirations. In the ages before him, the *summum bonum,* the highest good, was for the few. If it had ever been attained by humans at all, it had been attained only by an elite company of godlike men—great kings, chiefs, heroes, prophets, and holy men. The mass of humanity were destined for the underworld, or trapped on the wheel of rebirth. It was not for them to scale heaven. The Gods were jealous of their privileges, and admitted few to share them. The *summum bonum* might perhaps be attained by the masses; but then, only by the last generations, as in modern socialism, those who had died before being simply lost. There is no harrowing of hell in Marxism. But for Jesus every single human being is directly summoned to attain the highest good here and now, in the kingdom of God. When that has been preached, no further spiritual development can take us beyond it. A limit has been reached.

And Jesus' life is a final paradigm of man's relation to God, for he dramatically exemplifies the triumph and tragedy of faith: the triumph of rapturous communion with God in the assurance of God's love for men; and the tragedy of our relation to God, that we must nevertheless die and be utterly bereft of all that we have known of God and believed about him. He experienced the yes and the no of faith, the affirmation and the rejection of images, in a definitive way. To an icon-christology this is a scandal: but to me it is central.

Jesus' ethical teaching is final, in the sense that there can be no higher moral value than utter purity of heart, disinterestedness, and commitment to the way of love. There is not, and there cannot be, any higher moral value than this: again, it is ultimate, and cannot be superseded.

And Jesus' spirituality is final, in the sense that he all the time affirms, and yet in affirming transcends, the thought-situation in which he is set. An icon-christology cannot understand, and indeed usually ignores, the ever-present note of mocking irony in every recorded utterance of Jesus. Yet his irony is the clue to the understanding of Jesus, for it is his way of evoking the sense of the presence of God. He forces upon us a critical and questing spirit of restless dissatisfaction with all mundane values, institutions, and achievements, and a longing for that absolute good which we shall have to die to attain. It is, above all, through his ironical spirituality that he has imprinted his own distinctive vision upon mankind, and planted a seed of saving self-doubt in his Church. Christianity must never be allowed to become a mere religion, a positive symbolic system built around the idea of the incarnation. For it is infinitely more than that. It is a religion and a critique of religion, a religion which speaks of God by negating itself, which affirms a man who teasingly denied himself. Unfortunately the term 'antichrist' has already been pre-empted for another purpose: but Jesus is in truth both Messiah and antimessiah; for he never merely fulfils our aspirations, but invariably confounds them too: and it is in that ironical dialectic that he conveys his message.

The point of view I have outlined is based firmly on the Gospels, and the tradition of Jesus' own sayings as they have always been heard in the Church, and as they still stand in the light of modern biblical criticism. I affirm the finality of Christ in the sense that there can be no superseding of the central themes to which Jesus bears witness, nor any nobler way than his of bearing witness to them—the way of death. To claim iconic absoluteness for Jesus would subvert his message: how could men iconize an iconoclast without being aware of the absurd irony of their own mistake? But the finality I attribute to Jesus is not in any sense exclusive. Claims to exclusive finality have all too often been heard in Christianity, but any idea of exclusive property in divine truth is itself a manifestly ironical mistake.

12

THE CHRIST OF
CHRISTENDOM (1977)

The Eastern theologian John of Damascus (*c.* 675–749) once used a very curious argument in favour of icons. Ironically, it was because he was living under Muslim protection before Islam became generally iconoclastic that he was able to defend icons from within Islam at a time when it was not safe to defend them inside the Empire. John replied to the criticism that icons are unscriptural by admitting the fact, and adding that you will not find in scripture the Trinity or the *homoousion* or the two natures of Christ either. But we know *those* doctrines are true. And so, having acknowledged that icons, the Trinity and the incarnation are innovations, John goes on to urge his reader to hold fast to them as venerable traditions delivered to us by the fathers. If they were lost, the whole gospel would be threatened.

He was not the only one to use this argument: Theodore the Studite (759–826) adopted it too. It brings out an odd feature of Christianity, its mutability and the speed with which innovations come to be vested with religious solemnity to such an extent that anyone who questions them find *himself* regarded as the dangerous innovator and heretic. An amusing example from our own day is the assurance with which the church praises and defends 'the family' so that almost the first principle of Christian ethics is respect for the family and dutiful performance of one's assigned role in it. Yet the gospels are still canonical, and it appears from the gospels that Jesus was highly critical of the family for strong religious reasons. For him, the call of the kingdom was away from family roles, not into them. The idealization of the family is a modern cultural creation, which the churches have validated, and now no modern bishop would dream of publicly endorsing Jesus' views about the family.

It is perfectly possible for an opinion to be firmly believed to be orthodox, traditional, conservative and Catholic, when it is in fact of very recent origin. Yet the suggestion that the classical doctrine of the incarnation belongs, not to the essence of Christianity, but only to a certain period of church history, now ended, will certainly startle many people. Nevertheless, I believe it is true. To begin at the end, there was a certain moment in the nineteenth century when the old Chalcedonian 'orthodoxy', a view of Christ which had prevailed for fifteen hundred years, began to crumble from within. The last really able defence of a fully orthodox doctrine of Christ in Britain was H. P. Liddon's *The Divinity of our Lord and Saviour Jesus Christ*

(1865). The leader of the next generation, Charles Gore (1853–1932), found himself unable to continue the tradition.

It is important to remember that Gore really was an insider, for in these matters the thoughts of insiders are far more decisive than the thoughts of outsiders. In 'background', education, career and allegiances Gore was everything that the old bourgeois England, now passing away, thought a great churchman should be. As such he was of course no timeserver, but a thinker, an Anglo-Catholic, and a socialist, albeit of a very pale pink colour.

In his youth Gore seems to have been deeply influenced by reading Sir John Seeley's *Ecce Homo,* which had appeared in 1865. *Ecce Homo* was a pioneer in a *genre* still popular, the sentimental and by scholarly standards fictitious life of Jesus. Yet Gore, to the end of his life, thought it had real historical value, and it is remarkable to find him still praising it in 1927.[1] He belonged to a generation in which classical 'Mods and Greats' followed by private study of the Greek Testament and the Fathers still seemed a sufficient education for a theologian. He was no radical in biblical criticism and knew nothing of rabbinic Judaism. And for him *Ecce Homo* brought out something about the reality of Jesus' human life which the church had 'obscured'.

Gore's seniors, men like Liddon and E. B. Pusey, were contemptuous of *Ecce Homo,* and it is not immediately obvious why Gore was so impressed. He knew perfectly well, and always insisted, that the church had ever taught Christ's full humanity. He says rather priggishly that only divine providence could have led the fathers so firmly to emphasize Christ's manhood 'in an age when the general tendency of Catholic thought was certainly not humanitarian'.[2] And Gore never *intended* to break with orthodoxy, for he really did believe in the incarnation. He never believed that Jesus was a man with a human hypostasis ('person' in the technical sense, roughly equivalent to 'individuating principle' or 'distinct logical subject-of-predication', and rather narrower in meaning than 'individual spiritual substance'). Gore believed that in Jesus there was only one person, and that the person of the Word of God. So Jesus was not a man living a human life, but the divine Word living a human life. Gore did not learn from Seeley that Jesus was a man after all. Seeley led him to think that what had been lost was a full imaginative realization of what it was for the divine Word to have actually lived a *fully* human life.

Liddon asserted, and set out to prove, that there is no difference between history and dogma, that the Jesus of the gospels really was the Byzantine Christos Pantocrator, 'the God whom we believers adore'.[3] Gore would not say that there was a real conflict between the Jesus of the gospels and the

Christ of conciliar dogma, but he admitted a real distinction, and in effect a certain tension; and that was what mattered for the future.

His first manoeuvre was in line with Anglican tradition. He asserted that the old formulae (two natures, each entire, united without confusion in one divine person, coessential with Deity in his divine nature and with us in his human nature) did not contain any explanation of the incarnation, or analysis of its content, but merely defined certain limits to orthodox systematic thought and banned certain deviations from it. They set out not the content but the criteria of Catholic faith in Christ. They were not premises for dogmatic construction but rather boundaries within which it must keep.

Gore was making a form/matter distinction. To know the Word Incarnate you must do more than learn the definitions. You must read the gospels, guided by them. The dogmas prescribe the form, and the gospels provide the matter, of Christian knowledge of the incarnate Lord.

But if this were a sufficient answer, there would be no problem. The difficulty is, as Gore well knew, that if the orthodox dogma is internally incoherent it cannot function as a hedge, limit or boundary, because it fails to mark out and enclose any intelligible space for the Christian mind to move in. Gore was driven to tamper with the definitions in order to make them enclose such a real space.

Gore was not a philosophical theologian, and he did not phrase his questions in any very precise or technical form. He did not ask how one can distinguish, in God, between person, nature, and attributes belonging to that nature. He did not ask, in a technical way, how one can intelligibly affirm that a single subject, the divine Word, possesses three sets of attributes, the set which comprise his divine nature, the set which comprise essential human nature and a set of contingent human attributes, when some of the attributes in the first set appear to be incompossible in a single subject with some in the other two sets. He certainly did not ask how that being *can* be 'fully human', the metaphysical subject of whose life is not human, but divine. He did not put the matter in quite these technical terms. But he did implicitly raise such questions by the way he posed the particular issue of the incarnate Lord's human knowledge and consciousness.

Some commentators give the impression that Liddon had taught that Jesus was virtually omniscient, whereas Gore felt obliged to admit the limitation of Jesus' knowledge. This is misleading. What happened was that Gore found he could no longer hold together two things that Liddon *had* held together. Liddon, following tradition, declared that 'His Single Personality has two spheres of existence; in the one it is all-blessed, undying and omniscient; in the other it meets with pain of mind and body, with actual death, and with a corresponding liability to a limitation of knowledge'. But, says Liddon, 'these contrasts, while they enhance our sense of our Lord's love and condescension, do not destroy our apprehension of the Personal Unity of the Incarnate Christ'.[4] Liddon, that is, did not see in the full two-natures doctrine any threat to the unity of Christ's person. Gore did, and at this point begins to move away from Chalcedonian orthodoxy. Something he has learnt from *Ecce Homo* and from the gospels makes it impossible for him to see how the incarnate Lord can be fully human and *both* omniscient *and* ignorant. Quite clearly one thing that has happened is that whereas Liddon understands 'personality' in the traditional metaphysical sense. Gore is beginning to understand it in an historical, ethical and psychological sense. He talks mainly about Jesus' human consciousness, and the upshot of what he says is that he does *not* believe that the full panoply of divine attributes and all the attributes of humanity are co-present complete and entire, and where appropriate displayed, during the earthly life of the one person of the incarnate Lord. To save the unity of his person and the human entirety of his life, some of the divine attributes must be dimmed or veiled. The kenotic theory is the result.

I must emphasize that Gore did believe in the incarnation. A count in reasonably closely-matched passages suggests to me that Gore does not employ the term 'Jesus' any more than Liddon. Like Liddon, he prefers more honorific expressions like 'our Lord', 'Christ', 'Jesus Christ', 'the incarnate Lord', 'the Son of God' and so on. There is some linguistic shift, but it is not great; not as great as the same shift would be in a modern book. But he is moving away from the two-natures doctrine in its historic form. Thus he dislikes Pope Leo's Tome (of A.D. 449) which distributes to the Two Natures the words and deeds of Jesus, as if Jesus were at one moment merely Clark Kent and at the next Superman.[5] And if we object to Gore that he is 'psychologizing Jesus', he would surely have replied that Christian faith demands it, for it proposes a mutual sympathy between the believer and the Lord who condescended to share our sorrows.

Gore's kenotic theory is of merely historical interest now. He must describe an ethical, not a metaphysical, kenosis for the excellent reason that a metaphysical kenosis is incompatible with theism. Since the divine attributes belong to God not contingently but analytically it is logically impossible for the deity to doff one like a superfluous piece of clothing. But the ethical kenosis Gore describes (somewhat vaguely) is scarcely different from what may be found in Luther or Kierkegaard, or indeed Liddon himself. Besides which, the idea of kenosis in bourgeois Christian thought is clearly socially-conditioned. In a class society, where the Christian tradition was carried by people of very high status and privilege, there was a need for christological validation of the duty to 'condescend to men of low estate'. The change in the connotations of the word 'condescension' since those days gives us a revealing glimpse of theology's cultural relativity, and makes clear the hopeless inappropriateness of the idea of kenosis today.

But if Gore is remote from us, Liddon, the last defender of full orthodoxy, is a universe away. Liddon's Jesus is acutely aware of 'His rank in the scale of being', conscious of his own 'absolute sinlessness', speaks with 'intense authoritativeness' and 'increasing Self-assertion'. Indeed, for Liddon 'Self-assertion' is the dominant note in all Jesus' recorded teaching.[6] To read Liddon is to realize how far we have already travelled from full Chalcedonian orthodoxy. If Gore's Christ is that somewhat old-fashioned figure, a privileged person with an earnest social conscience, Liddon's Christ is a completely confident authoritarian monarch, the Christ of Christendom.

My suggestion is then that the themes of the present volume are not novel, even in a conservative country like Britain. Somewhere between Liddon and Gore a view of Christ which took shape in the fourth and fifth centuries began to collapse; and to collapse, not just in the minds of rationalist critics, but in the minds of the leading churchmen of the day. And if social and political changes at least partly account for its breakdown, they were correspondingly involved in its rise.

For if the 'orthodox' doctrine of Christ had an end, it also had a beginning. We can gain some idea of the character of that beginning by considering one or two moments in the history of Christian art.

The Bible contains (Exodus 20.4) a categorical prohibition, not merely of any kind of image of God, but of any naturalistic or representational art, a prohibition which has influenced Jews and Muslims to this day. Nothing other than God can be an adequate image of God, and God himself, being transcendent, cannot be delineated. Early Christianity inherited and followed this rule. Old Testament arguments against idolatry, pagan arguments and early Christian arguments ran closely parallel.[7]

Preconstantinian Christian art was scarce, unofficial, of very poor quality and often somewhat ambiguous. Many a pagan sculptured frieze might incorporate the figures of a philosopher, holding a codex, with his disciples; or of a youthful shepherd, or a vine. There was just enough Christian art in the West for the Latin writer Tertullian to take the trouble to denounce the practice of portraying the Good Shepherd, but, Tertullian being what he was, that does not amount to much.

Even in the fourth century Christian art as it began to emerge met very sharp traditionalist opposition. The Emperor Constantine's sister wrote to Bishop Eusebius of Caesarea, requesting a portrait of Christ. Few prelates have ever been more obsequious to royalty than Eusebius, but he sharply refused her request, explaining the biblical and traditional grounds for the church's detestation of idolatry. Christian art, he says, doesn't exist and cannot exist. In 343 Cyril, Bishop of Jerusalem, attacked the portrayal of the crucifixion in his Easter Sermon; and later still (c. 380) Bishop Epiphanius of Salamis, visiting Palestine, was so enraged to see a church hanging with a figure of Christ or a saint that he tore it down, and subsequently delivered himself of a fiercely polemical treatise against icons, which he regarded as idols.

But the protests of these great churchmen were in vain: Christian art was emerging as part of a complex process by which Christianity was very extensively paganized in its faith, worship, organization and social teaching. The period during which the classical doctrine of Christ was being framed was also the period in which a largely pagan iconography of Christ was developed; and these developments were both of them profoundly influenced by political needs and pressures.

N. H. Baynes, in a brief article on 'Eusebius and the Christian Empire',[8] showed how very closely Eusebius' first sketch of the political theology of Byzantium followed the Hellenistic philosophy of kingship. As God is to the cosmos, so the king is to the state. The divine logos indwells the king, teaching him to mimic the divine virtue, to be a good shepherd of his people, to save them from sin and lead them by the path of salvation to the heavenly kingdom. The king was a kind of incarnate god, the one link between earth and heaven.

To 'Christianize' this scheme it was only necessary to declare Christ the universal cosmic Emperor, and make the earthly Emperor his servant and vicar. The entire imperial cult and ideology was refocused on Christ, while in return Christ crowned his earthly deputy and validated his rule. Eusebius took only the first step in this direction, but others soon followed.

In the new order, the church's chief ministers were granted secular dignity, privileges, dress and insignia, much of which they tenaciously maintain to this day, and the church's worship borrowed extensively from court ritual. And all this, says Theodore Klauser, 'served to transform permanently the way in which the person of Jesus Christ was represented. . . . [He] began to be looked on as a ruler who as the "Pantocrator" governed the whole of creation . . . he assumed the outward marks of imperial rank; he was the ruler who sat on a throne adorned with jewels and purple cushions, who wore the royal halo, whose foot and hand were kissed, who was surrounded with a heavenly cortege of palace officials and much else besides'. Almost the only remaining trace of Jesus is his dark bearded Semitic face, peering out with understandable sadness from its incongruous new setting. His associates were similarly exalted: 'Mary became the Mother and Empress, the apostles were turned into a senate, the angels now constituted the household of a heavenly court, and the saints were represented as guests seeking audience and bringing their offerings.'[9]

All this is familiar enough, and is exhibited more eloquently at Ravenna, or in a pontifical high mass, or in a coronation service, than ever it could be in words. Early Christianity had repudiated the Emperor-cult, but now conciliar Christianity came increasingly to be modelled on the Emperor-cult. It is scarcely surprising that the Emperors saw the correct definition of the dogma of Christ as a matter of high political importance; and when it was defined to their satisfaction they enforced it with all the power of the State, establishing a political order which in one form and another lingered on until the First World War.

Now it might be that in spite of the dubious political circumstances of its definition, the orthodox dogma of the incarnation might nonetheless be true. But in fact I believe that the way the dogma came to be defined had in the long run damaging effects upon belief in God, and upon the way man's relation to God was conceived. Four arguments will, I hope, make the point clear.

1. The assertion that deity itself and humanity are permanently united in the one person of the incarnate Lord suggests an ultimate synthesis, a conjunction and continuity between things divine and things of this world. As the popular maxim had it, Grace does not destroy but perfects Nature.

This idea distorts Jesus' message. Christianity's proper subtlety and freedom depended upon Jesus' ironical perception of *disjunction* between the things of God and the things of men, a disjunction particularly enforced in the parables, as distinct from similitudes, allegories and analogies.[10] Whether he is seen as an apocalyptic prophet or as a witty rabbi (or, as I think, both), what matters in Jesus' message is his sense of the abrupt juxtaposition of two opposed orders of things. The way things seem from one point of view is the opposite of the way they seem from the other. This emphasis on *contrasting* value-scales evokes the transcendent, and it underlies Jesus' paradoxes of righteousness and unrighteousness, loss and gain, death and life, poverty and riches, the manifest and the hidden, security and insecurity, prudence and folly, and justice and injustice. The essential thing is that the two contrasting orders must collide.

But the doctrine of the incarnation unified things which Jesus had kept in ironic contrast with each other, and so weakened the ability to appreciate his way of speaking, and the distinctive values he stood for. In a terminology I have used elsewhere, instead of a negative and indirect christology there was developed an icon-christology, the parables came to be seen as allegories, and disjunctions were turned into continuities. A world-view which expressed disjunction and free choice was exchanged for a world-view which stressed continuity, hierarchy and due obedience. For example, in biblical and early Christian thought Jesus' kingship is different in kind from, indeed the moral opposite of, gentile kingship. But in Christendom that distinction was lost. Christ crowned the Emperor, one a step higher in the scale of being merely stooping slightly to bestow authority upon one a step lower.[11] In the Christian iconography which ran from the late fourth century to the end of the Byzantine period Christ and the Emperor were virtually indistinguishable, and the theologians themselves declared the veneration of icons of the former to be precisely on a par with the veneration of tokens of the latter.[12] Christ's lordship was originally eschatological, and manifest in this age only indirectly and by ironic *contrast* with temporal lordship. But the dogma of the incarnation brought it forward into this present age. As the manifest Absolute in history, Christ became the basis of the Christian Empire and of political and ecclesiastical power in the present age. He was invoked to guarantee the very things Jesus had said were passing away. Delicate theological distinctions and contrasts such as are made in the Johannine dialogue between Christ and Pilate (John 18.33–19.16) and in Matthew 20.20–28, Luke 22.24–27, were as a result lost. Inevitably Christianity became, or rather was deliberately made, absolutist and authoritarian. The Jewishness of Jesus' teaching was lost, and has never since been allowed to influence christology. Almost the only human trait that was retained was the *philanthropia* which he shared with the ideal Hellenistic king.

A vivid illustration of this engrained habit of turning from the Jews to the Greeks is Rudolf Bultmann's explicit relegation of Jesus to the history of Judaism. Bultmann simply expels Jesus from Christianity as an irrelevance, and brazenly treats Christ as an ecclesiastical creation only tenuously linked with Jesus. This is all the more odd in that Bultmann's teaching about God is so impressive. Why cannot he see that the Jewish Jesus he rejects is a shrewder and more cunning witness to God than is his empty ecclesiastical Christ? Presumably he cannot see it because, as Hegel once put it, Judaea cannot and must not be the Teutons' fatherland; and because he is convinced that the heart of the gospel lies in Lutheran dogma rather than in the tradition of Jesus' own teaching. If that tradition were to be taken seriously, Chalcedon and later dogmatic systems derived from it would have to be abandoned in favour of a fresh start.

The point here is related to the old question of the infallibility of scripture. Fundamentalists regard scripture as the words of God and spend a great deal of time studying it, but totally fail to understand it. Their doctrinal view of scripture cuts them off from its reality. When scripture is regarded as the unitary expression of one absolute mind, its internal diversity and richness cannot be recognized. The same is true of Jesus. Just as a 'deabsolutized' scripture is of infinitely greater religious value than the flat oracle of fundamentalism, so a 'deabsolutized' Jesus can be recognized as revealing God to us in much more complex ways than the Christ of Chalcedon. If it was a religious gain to get rid of an absolutist view in the one case, it will be so also in the other. The transformation of our attitude in the one case must in the long run demand a corresponding transformation in the other. I believe the result will be a clearer grasp of the truth about God and Jesus, and of distinctively Christian values which have for long been obscured.

2. Orthodox doctrine asserts that the divine and the human are indissolubly united in the person of the divine Word, with effect from the moment of Christ's conception. This appears to assert that the union of God with man was miraculously accomplished by God independently of, because prior to, the struggles and suffering of Jesus' earthly life, which thus become peripheral. To this, two replies might be made, but neither is entirely satisfactory.

Orthodox dyotheletism claims that there is real and meritorious moral struggle in Jesus' life, because there are in him two wills, one human, the other divine. But the claim that in the incarnate Lord a divine will for which sin is a logical impossibility is hypostatically united with a human will for which it is a real and pressing temptation raises all the difficulties which Gore, as we saw above, felt so strongly.

In the second place, some early theologians appear to suggest[13] that the hypostatic union was dissolved upon the death of Jesus. His body was in the tomb, his soul in the underworld and the Logos reigned on in heaven. The hypostatic union was restored at the resurrection. But, though this theory certainly emphasizes the reality of Christ's passion, it clearly had to be rejected, for it suggests that death *can* after all put asunder what God has joined. In which case my question about whether the traditional dogma does justice to Jesus' human striving to bring men to God and God to men returns. In the traditional language, is the Chalcedonian doctrine compatible with a full recognition of Christ's priestly and mediatorial office?

3. If in Jesus the fullness of God himself is permanently incarnate, Jesus can be directly worshipped as God without risk of error or blasphemy. A cult of Christ as distinct from a cult of God thus becomes defensible, and did in fact develop. The practice of praying direct to Christ in the Liturgy, as distinct from praying to God through Christ, appears to have originated among the innovating 'orthodox' opponents of Arianism in the fourth century.[14] It slowly spread, against a good deal of opposition, eventually to produce Christocentric piety and theology. An example of the consequent paganization of Christianity was the agreement to constitute the World Council of Churches upon the doctrinal basis of 'acknowledgment of our Lord Jesus Christ as God and Saviour'—and nothing else.[15] Perhaps it was only when Christocentric religion finally toppled over into the absurdity of 'Christian Atheism' that some Christians began to realize that Feuerbach

might have been right after all; Chalcedonian christology could be a remote ancestor of modern unbelief, by beginning the process of shifting the focus of devotion from God to man. It could not put up any resistance to the focusing of piety upon the glory of the incarnate Lord rather than the glory of God, and then upon the humanity of Christ, and then upon humanity in general. On the contrary, it appeared to legitimate a cult of humanity. Similarly, it could not resist the giving of the title *Theotokos,* Mother of God, to Mary. The phrase 'Mother of God' is *prima facie* blasphemous, but it has had a very long run and the orthodox have actively promoted its use, fatally attracted by its very provocativeness.

4. If it is the case that in the incarnation God himself has permanently assumed human nature, and can legitimately be depicted as God in human form, then eventually the ultimate mystery of deity will be conceived anthropomorphically, and the pagan notion of a deity as a superhuman person with gender will be restored. In due course this happened, aided by the traditional Father-Son imagery.

The Eastern Church was for long stricter in this matter than the Western. The nearest it came to permitting the Deity to be portrayed *in a human form different from the human form of Christ* was in the standard iconography of such a scene as the Baptism of Christ, where a hand, but no more than hand, emerges from the cloud to release the dove upon the Lord's head.[16] It was also permissible to portray the 'Old Testament Trinity' of Genesis 18.[17] There are some, highly exceptional, early representations of God: a miniature in the Smyrna Octateuch, a Paternity (depicting God the Father and God the Son as two men) in an eleventh-century Constantinopolitan codex; but such things are rare. Strictly, God remained unportrayable until in the early sixteenth century, and under Western influence, images of him appeared in Moscow.[18] A layman, Djak Viskovaty, deserves to be remembered for having lodged a formal and well-documented protest in 1553/4. Unfortunately, the synod found against him, and though the decision went the other way in 1667, images of God the Father subsequently became common, especially in peasant icons.

The Western story is rather different. The whole religious style from early times emphasized instruction by narrative rather than the symbolic representation of timeless truth. But for centuries, in accordance with both orthodox theology and iconographical rules, the image of God the Son was used to represent the God of the Old Testament when illustrating Genesis, or the visions of the prophets. It was clearly recognized (as at the time when the 'Caroline Books' were written, c. 790–2) that there are limits to Christian art. Just when these limits were transgressed is hard to discover exactly. Searching has persuaded me that one can only be quite certain, without the risk of misinterpretation, in the case of a single work of art unmistakably representing the Trinity, in which God the Father's human form is present alongside that of the Son, and is distinctly *different*. This rules out such images as the drawings in the Sherborne Pontifical described by Francis Wormald.[19] On my criterion, anthropomorphic images of God the Father become increasingly common after about 1100.[20]

It is not often realized what a theological monstrosity such images are; but if Deity itself has a human form already, prior to the incarnation, then the latter *must* be understood in a pagan way. Again, the absurdity comes out clearly in the common practice of using *two* men to portray Christ, one standing for his human nature and the other for his divine nature. The early work of art in which all these oddities are combined is the 'The Quinity of Winchester', now in Warsaw, which depicts three men, a woman and a bird—God the Father and his Eternal Son in a Paternity group, the Virgin and her child the incarnate Son in his human nature, and the dove nesting in her crown—all in one group.[21]

The emergence of God as an old man in the Western Christian imagination is, on the evidence of the history of art, a many-stranded process. One likely source of it is the Paternity group, modelled on the old theme of the Virgin and child, from which are derived the standard images of the Trinity at the baptism of Christ and the crucifixion. And it is my contention that the doctrine of Christ as God's divine Son has here humanized deity to an intolerable degree. The strangeness of it is seldom noticed even to this day. A sensitive theologian like Austin Farrer can dwell eloquently upon a medieval icon of the Trinity,[22] and a philosopher as gifted as Wittgenstein can discuss Michelangelo's painting of God in the Sistine Chapel,[23] and in neither case is it noticed that there *could* be people to whom such pagan anthropomorphism is abhorrent, because it signifies a 'decline of religion' in the only sense that really matters, namely, a serious corruption of faith in God.

In recent years Freudians and feminists (arguing very different cases) have assumed that the God of monotheistic faith is male. It sounds like a theological solecism on their part, but it is surely an excusable solecism, in view of the long tradition of extreme and barbarous anthropomorphism in Western art. The Council of Trent (Sessio XXV, 3 and 4 December 1563) defended images of Christ and the saints on the old grounds laid down by Gregory I, but simply failed to comment on images of God the Father. Such images have never been officially defended in the West, it is true; but they were tolerated, and the old faith was forgotten.

From all this I conclude that the doctrine of the incarnation has had some harmful effects upon the understanding of Jesus' message, on the understanding of his relation to God and even upon faith in God. For Jesus' emphasis upon the divine transcendence, on the disjunction of things divine and human and the need for choice, it substituted a world-view which stressed continuity, authority and due obedience (1). It weakened appreciation of his human work (2). It tended to create a cult of the divine Christ which let Deity itself fade into the background (3), and when God the Father was reaffirmed, he was envisaged as an old man (4).

What we have been taught to call 'orthodoxy' was in fact merely the form of Christianity which happened to triumph over the others. In retrospect, the Christ of the Eastern Church looks all too like the Hellenistic king exalted to heaven to become the ideological basis of the Christian Empire; and the Christ of the Western Church looks like one who died to seal the authority of the patriarchal family as a model for the organization of church and state. Neither Christ was Jesus, and neither reveals the one true God as Jesus did; and the political order with which conciliar orthodoxy was associated has now passed away for ever.

The discovery that the ecclesiastical Christ is not to be found in a critical reading of the records of Jesus led to scepticism about the historicity of the gospels. This scepticism served to protect the ecclesiastical Christ from historical refutation. But the figure behind the gospels is not quite unreachable. As enough remains of the Buddha to challenge the Mahayana so *a fortiori* enough remains of Jesus to challenge us to rethink our ideas of Christ. In doing so we will be furthering the theological task of the modern period, that of shifting Christianity from the dogmatic faith of the Christendom period to the critical faith which is to succeed it. Of course the shift from the dogmatic to the critical outlook is difficult, but it will not take us further from Jesus: it will bring us closer to him. It will enable us to *recover* truths which have been largely lost.

In this paper I have criticized the 'orthodox' view of Christ on various counts: that it 'realized' eschatology (i.e. brought forward ultimate things into the present age) so far as to validate this-worldly sovereignty and to politicize the transcendent, that it constantly tended towards anthropocentrism, and so on. But readers may still fear that the drift of the argument is such as to leave no room for a religiously-adequate Christology—one, that is, which does full justice to the conviction that God was in Christ, reconciling the world to himself, committing himself in the midst of the human to redeem the human.

The objection is deeply felt, but I believe it is properly met by the insistence that the doctrine of Christ must be such as to strengthen and purify, not to compromise, our understanding of the divine transcendence. For it is the divine *transcendence* which alone judges, delivers and restores, as Jesus, in his teaching and in his person, communicates the power of transcendence (the Holy Spirit) to his disciples. God is with man, in man, only in his transcendence. The criterion of religious adequacy, rightly understood, itself demands that christology be not any kind of man-cult: it must be theocentric, not christocentric.

APPENDIX

I relegate a bold hypothesis to an appendix. Iconographically, Christ is the Emperor, and the Father the Pope. God the Father emerges as a common theme in Christian art in the eleventh and twelfth centuries. His seniority is stressed: he is above and behind the Son, older, heavier in appearance. There may be a connection here with the Papacy's growing claims and confidence after Hildebrand. Certainly trinitarian images of the latter Middle Ages look like statements about papal authority.

Theologically, the representation of the Father and the Son as two different persons had important effects on the doctrine of the atonement from Anselm onwards. It became a transaction between an eternal Father and his eternal Son, a transaction which (envisaged as it was in anthropomorphic and indeed psychological terms) was bound in the end to occasion a moral revolt.

13

RELIGIOUS HUMANISM (1991)

The word "humanism" is so well-established and familiar to us that it comes as a surprise to learn that it is a theological term of recent origin, having been introduced by Samuel Taylor Coleridge. He meant by it the doctrine, held for example by Unitarians, that affirms only the humanity of Christ. Later in the nineteenth century the term came to be used of Auguste Comte's "Religion of Humanity". This was a secular religion modelled on Catholicism, which worshipped Humanity as symbolised by the figure of a mother and child. A fully modern use of the word "humanism" perhaps begins only in the early twentieth century. It comes from the American pragmatists F. C. S. Schiller and William James.

According to Schiller, "Humanism . . . is merely the perception that the philosophic problem concerns human beings striving to comprehend a world of human experience by the resources of human minds" (cited from the *Oxford English Dictionary,* Supplement Volume 2, 1976, "humanism"). Schiller means something like this: since Antiquity we have been deeply influenced both by the religious doctrine that the human mind is made in the image of the divine Mind, and by the philosophical doctrine that regards the human mind as having access to, or participating in, a cosmic and time-less order of intelligibility and values. The combined influence of Genesis and Plato produced a certain super-naturalism of reason and conscience. *We* believed that our intellectual and moral faculties somehow lifted us right out of nature. But in the light of modern knowledge, that view is no longer tenable. Evolutionary biology and the historical and social sciences have brought us down to earth, reminding us that our thinking and valuing are just human and serve practical human proposes. We are always inside our human situation and our human point of view: we don't outsoar it altogether, as the older doctrine seemed to imply. Pragmatists are therefore suspicious of grandiose talk about *a priori* reason and eternal truth. They emphasise instead that we are practical animals who live in time, with lives to live and needs to be met. Our knowledge-systems and our moralities have been developed to serve the purposes of life in this world, here and now.

All this seems to imply a contrast. On the one hand, a humanism which is secular, practical, this-worldly, and constantly revising its hypotheses in response to change. And on the other hand, a religious and philosophi-cal tradition which was monkish, contemplative and orientated towards a heavenly world of unchanging perfection. And it is true, I think, that in our European tradition the human did first emerge and assert itself in distinction from what was sacred and divine. From the Renaissance, a "Humanist" was a person who studied "human letters", which meant the classics of Latin and Greek Antiquity, in contrast with the dominant study of "sacred letters", which meant Scripture and divinity. In places like the church of Santa Croce, Florence, one can see the tombs of some of the early Italian Humanists, and it is noticeable that they have virtually no Christian language or symbolism upon them.

This may give the impression that humanism and religion could easily become opposites: and so it has often been in the twentieth-century debate. It is as if we want the other person to be the inverted image of ourselves, the necessary opponent. Christians are concerned with things spiritual, therefore humanists must be materialistic. Christians take a pessimistic view of human nature, therefore humanists must be optimistic. Since they don't worship God, humanists must presumably worship Man. And humanists for their part do the same sort of thing in the opposite direction. We are this-worldly, so Christians must be other-worldly. We trust reason, they trust faith. We are willing to review our beliefs in the light of experience; they are dogmatists who defy the evidence. And so on: we relish this sort of adversarial thinking. It helps us to draw the battle-lines and polarise the issues.

However, people like us should be suspicious of popular and conventional binary oppositions. I want to make the case the other way, by insisting that strong currents of Greek philosophy and ethics, and of this-worldly and humanistic thinking, have run within the Christian tradition since Biblical times. There is very little evidence of platonism or monasticism in the Bible, and Christianity can easily be turned in a humanistic, materialistic and this-worldly direction. There is plenty to justify such a turn in the Bible itself.

First, within the Hebrew Bible there is a Jewish humanism that is older than either Greek or Christian humanism. In the Patriarchal narratives and in the Court History of David (Genesis and I and II Samuel) we already find a style of writing that can only be called prose fiction. In these texts God and the supernatural are in the background. In the foreground there is a drama of human relationships. The character and fate of the individual are formed and revealed through his and her interactions with others in a purely human world. Fiction is a rather feminist medium in which strong women characters can emerge, so it is noticeable that, of the seven or so ancient Jewish books that are commonly admitted to be fictional, four bear the names of women: Ruth, Esther, Judith, and Susanna. (The others I am counting are Job, Tobit, and Bel and the Dragon.)

Secondly, there is a very strong tendency in the Hebrew Bible, both in the Torah and in the Prophets, to equate holiness with righteousness, and the daily practice of religion with social ethics.

Thirdly, the ancient Jewish understanding of the human being was in many ways closer to pragmatism than to platonism. There is little or no evidence of body-soul dualism, life after death, a timeless eternity, or pure abstract thought. Thinking happened in the heart, not the brain, and was closely linked to action. The whole vision of life was this-worldly and dramatic.

Fourthly, already in the Hebrew Bible—in Hosea, Jeremiah, and some of the Psalms, for example—we hear someone who speaks in the first person in tones of lament, plea, confession, testimony, and so forth. This is the beginning of a tradition of spiritual autobiography, and of interest in the drama of subjective religious life, which continues in the texts of Paul and Augustine and eventually becomes one of the glories of the West. No other religion has produced so much autobiography and biography, and no other culture-area has made so much of the formation, the psychology and the fate of the individual human self. We may sometimes think that the Western self is too divided and self-accusing; but at any rate it is interesting, and it is a sign that our religious tradition has done more than any other to make the life of the ordinary human being seem important.

Many of the themes that I have so far mentioned are continued and further developed in the New Testament. Jesus in the Parables continues the fictional tradition that equates the religious realm with the world of everyday life and personal relationships, Paul continues the autobiographical tradition, and so on. But in addition there are three new themes to which I must draw attention.

The first new theme is the very familiar one of the Incarnation and Pentecost. In Christ God has entered the human world and has even become our fellow human being. In the Spirit God has poured himself out into the flux of human relationships. So the Trinity is a symbol of the death of God, that is, of God's self-giving and his disappearance into the human realm.

The second new theme in the New Testament is the internalisation of Christ's suffering and death within the believer, so that the Christian's psychological conflict and stress become the labour-pains of a new humanity in a new world. Of course, too, the close association of love with pain in Christianity means that the faith has always been somewhat sado-masochistic. And no doubt these are real disadvantages. But they bring with them the most complex and rich dramatics of selfhood that the human race has yet developed.

Finally, the third theme is the end of religion. In the Bible religion is not an end in itself. Religion is only a disciplinary institution which operates in the historical period, between the expulsion of humankind from Eden and the arrival of the New Jerusalem. Religion is a Law, a system of rituals and constraints which is authoritative during the period of waiting for our final redemption. Now, by proclaiming the arrival of the Kingdom of God, Jesus was in effect promising the end of religion. When he arrives, the old absolutes of religion suddenly become merely relative and transient. The liberation of human beings that he promises will be a liberation not just from sin but also from the religious institutions that were set up to limit the effects of sin. That is why Jesus can say things like: "The sabbath was made for man, not man for the sabbath; so the Son of Man is lord even of the sabbath." The institutions of religion are only tools, and have only an interim function.

Thus at the very beginning of Christianity there was a promise that the age of religion was coming to an end. Religion was in process of transcending itself into the pure humanism of the New Covenant.

In the light of all this I think we now see why so many of the great nineteenth-century thinkers regarded Christianity as a profoundly humanistic faith, and one that in our own time is naturally evolving into secular humanism. So the question now becomes: "Why do we need to keep any links with religion **and** religious practice at all? Why don't we just become straight secular humanists?"

My answer is this: because it is so humanistic, our tradition is profoundly historical. It has lived through many profound cultural upheavals, and it is living through one now. At such times, all our ideas go into the melting-pot. Our vision of the world and our moral and intellectual standards are not exempt. They are themselves cultural products. We have no access to anything that is unaffected by historical change. But this means that we haven't got permanent and unchanging concepts of human nature, or of rationality or of morality. As a result, the various Enlightenment, liberal and Marxist versions of humanism have broken down.

In this situation, after nihilism, we need the religious imagination and the practice of religion to help us to re-fiction ourselves. It is an ongoing task. Nothing tells us what a human being is, and nothing dictates our values. We have got to make it all up. So I practise faith, I go over the old myths and re-enact the old rituals, and I try to add a little bit to the tradition, because I now see religion as supplying us with the schooling and the symbols we need for this new task of ours. We have to keep on reimagining ourselves, our values and our world.

In the past, people always did fiction the meaning of their own lives. Whole societies did it communally, and the result was what we call religion. It was evolved unconsciously, like a tradition of folk art. In the future we have got to do the same job consciously, and keep on doing it. Because we do it consciously, it will be a sort of humanism, but because we know we still need communal myths and rituals, it will also be religion. We shall be religious humanists, making believe.

Part Four

Success and Failure

in Religion

14

AN APOLOGIA FOR MY
THINKING (2002)

All my writing has been an attempt to explain myself, but I don't seem to have succeeded very well, because so many people continue to say, 'Yes, yes, but now could you please explain in words of one syllable what you've been trying to do for all these years?' So I must try again.

Since the age of about fifteen I have known that I am a person unusually preoccupied with philosophical and religious questions, and especially the sort of questions that are called 'existential'. What are we; what sort of sense can we make of our world and the way we are placed in it; and what is the best that we can hope and aim for? For about fifty years I have wanted to reach, and to state in a book, a view about these matters with which I could feel content. Usually I have put the point by saying: 'I'd like to write a really truthful religious book'.

I started with Christian faith, to which I became committed at the age of fifteen, and with two great systems of thought to which I was introduced at school—platonism and darwinism. Plato's philosophy, with which Christian theology has almost always been intertwined, is the greatest example of a 'top-down', or metaphysical, account of reality. The apparent world in which we live is explained by reference to a greater unseen and controlling 'spiritual' or 'intelligible' world above. Our dual nature—body and soul, the passions and reason—shows that a part of us properly belongs to that higher world. Our life is then a journey through time towards the last home in eternity which we hope to enter through death.

That was impressive, but darwinism was equally impressive, for it was and it still remains the most wonderful and potent demonstration of the sheer power of purely 'immanent' and gradualistic or 'naturalistic' explanation. Just time and chance and the natural process of things, over sufficient time, can give rise to astonishingly complex and self-maintaining objects such as the housefly on the wall, your brain and our language.

Although darwinism is, as some people like to insist, 'only a scientific theory', its implications are formidable. If Darwin is right, there seems to be no need to postulate any special divine action in order to account for the first appearance, and the capacities, of human beings in the world. But Darwin obviously *is* right on the main issue. Has he not then made God redundant? Christian platonism could, to some extent, cope with this by pointing out that it has always preferred to play down talk of a personal God and his intervention in the world, describing all such language as merely 'analogical' or symbolic. But more seriously, as the darwinian style of purely-immanent explanation spreads out from biology into other subjects, it seems more and more to make obsolete any talk of an unseen metaphysical order behind the visible world. We are not embodied souls: we are just talking animals.

Philosophers usually don't like to admit that a mere scientific theory could be of such enormous intellectual importance; but the fact is that darwinism has probably been the chief influence in bringing about the Death of God and the end of metaphysics.

In my own case, the conflict in my thinking between platonism and darwinism was eventually resolved after thirty years, when first I put forward in 1980 the non-realist doctrine of God, and then in subsequent books extended non-realism through my philosophy generally.

The non-realist doctrine of God is fairly close to Kant's teaching. We should give up the old realistic idea of God as an infinite, all-powerful Person-out-there who controls all world-events, but we can keep the idea of God as 'the pearl of great price', a spiritual ideal and the focus of the religious life. To say that God is love is in effect to say simply that love is God; and although a purely ideal God doesn't push, he can still have considerable pulling-power. So in the Eighties I used to say that believing in God is by no means the same thing as thinking that God 'exists'. Talk about God doesn't give us any metaphysical information: it functions to guide the spiritual life.

So far, so good. I planned to keep the practical and religious use of the idea of God, whilst dispensing with the old metaphysical God out there who orders and unifies the world and knows everything as it really is. But in the following years my non-realism spread from God to become a general philosophical position, and everything began to shift and crumble. If there is no absolute Mind out there and no metaphysical order, then there are no objective and timeless essences or meanings for us to think in. There is no 'mentalese' or abstract language of pure thought. Human thinking becomes merely a way of talking to oneself in the current vernacular language. We can think only in the public language—which means that thinking is not something spiritual and basic but something secondary. If there is no Mind out-there that makes, knows and unifies everything, then there is no Cosmos; no ready-made, orderly and intelligible world out there. There is no absolute vision of *the* world; there is only *our* world, the world-picture painted by our current theory. And because our language and our theory are not anchored, but are changing all the time, we are always stuck within our own merely-human angles upon our world. Because we can never think outside our own shifting language, we can never be sure of objective reality or truth. As Nietzsche says bluntly: 'There are no facts, only interpretations'.

In effect, every single subject studied in the modern *poly*versity is a field of discourse on which conflicting interpretations jostle against each other, and 'truth' can never be more than today's state of play. And that's as true of religion and ethics as it is of every other subject. Value is only current market value, and meaning is only current usage.

In Nietzsche's day the worlds of music and the theatre were beginning to grasp, for the first time, the implications of the rule that 'Every performance is an interpretation'. Musicians and theatre directors may go on producing fresh interpretations of classical works till the end of history, but nobody will ever produce the final and definitive interpretation that makes any further reinterpretations unnecessary. Playing his works on an organ just like his will not by itself gives us the 'real' J. S. Bach, and the quest of the historical Jesus will not by itself lead us to the essence of Christianity. Interpretation or 'spin' goes all the way down, and we never get to a pure uninterpreted essence of the thing.

Thus as we explore its implications non-realism unpicks the world, leaving us with no absolute Origin, no last End and no objective reality, or value, or truth. It leaves us with only a beginningless, endless and outsideless flux of conflicting interpretations; and since the whole analysis applies to us too, we ourselves are also melted down into the general flux. Hence my recent phrase: 'Empty radical humanism'. There is nothing but *our* language, *our* world, and the meanings and truths and interpretations that *we* have generated. The world fully becomes the world, bright and conscious of itself, only in us and as *our* world. We are the only worldbuilders; but we are as empty as our world. In the end, there is only emptiness and brightness, as in a late-Monet painting of vegetation and water. Beautiful, but—I must admit—ultralight.

Along these lines I moved during the 1980s from a rather cautious and conservative non-realism about God, towards a form of 'nihilism'. But this wasn't as pessimistic and gloomy a progression as you may suppose. After all, I loved the analogous movement in painting, from realism to impressionism and on eventually to abstraction in Kandinsky and Mondrian. I had two main arguments for optimism: one was that what we made, we can remake. Old-fashioned conservative realists always like to say that things such as 'human nature' or 'God's revelation' are fixed and can't be changed by us; but I could reply that if we ourselves have evolved amongst ourselves our own pictures of everything, then anything and everything can be changed. What we made, we can remake. Thus non-realism makes an optimistic utopian outlook possible again. And secondly, when my 'active non-realism' reduces us also to being no more than transient bits of the general flux of things, it thereby helps us to feel completely at one with the world of which we are parts. A religious person no longer has to feel that she's exiled from her true home in another world. On the contrary, we can feel completely at home, now, this minute, and in this world. More generally, personal fulfilment and the point of our life are not to be sought either in a mythical Beginning or in a mythical End of all things, but simply here and now, and in the present moment. Thus my non-realism eventually led me to what I now call 'solar ethics', a spirituality of creative self-expression in the present moment.

So much for the way my philosophy was developing during the Eighties. In theology, I was in 1980 still close to the existentialist theologians—people like Bultmann and Tillich. For these thinkers, each Christian doctrine was to be understood in terms of the attitude to life that it prescribed. Thus to believe in God as our Creator was to understand that you should treat your own existence as a pure and gracious gift, and to believe in God's Providence was to believe that if we stick to our faith, we will in the end come through. When I live a risen life, Christ is risen—in me; and when Christ's teaching rules my life, he is ascended—in me. So I didn't actually *change* the doctrines very much at all. I just translated them into rules of life, as Wittgenstein had said one should do.

By the end of the Eighties, however, as I moved into all-out postmodernism, I was claiming the latitude to borrow religious symbols and themes and to reinterpret them in whatever way seemed to be necessary. The notion of an endless flux of conflicting interpretations after all applies as much to the Bible and the Christian tradition as to anything else, and I was feeling the need to take advantage of it, so that I could drastically reinterpret tradition. It was beginning to be clear that Christianity as we have received it is collapsing very rapidly, and we are moving into a revolutionary situation.

After 1991, then, I gave up officiating in church—though to this day I remain a communicant—and I began to talk about Post-Christianity, or alternatively 'Kingdom theology'. The main idea is that we now need to move beyond the ecclesiastical version of Christianity that we have known hitherto. Church-Christianity has a strong authority-structure. It is disciplinary, based on faith in supernatural doctrine, and very strongly oriented towards either life after death, or the Second Coming of Christ. In all these respects, it is now historically obsolete—the main reason being that since the death of communism and of the belief in progress, we have quickly lost all remaining forms of the idea that it is worth putting up with hard times now for the sake of a much better and greater world that is yet to come. Instead, we need what I call 'solar ethics', or kingdom religion. It is a way of committing oneself completely and unreservedly to life, through which we can find 'eternal' happiness (a happiness that never fails us, however bad things get to be) in the present moment. We can't trust doctrine and we can't trust promises about the future: religion must deliver *now*.

This last stage in my thinking was first sketched in 1994/5, and has been further elaborated in a flurry of books since 1996. There have been three or four new themes. In *After God* (1996) I sketched a philosophy of our religious history which aimed to show how in traditional society religious ideas functioned to stabilize the whole 'Symbolic Order'; that is, the whole world of language. A society oriented towards change, like ours, will not need the older kind of religion any more. In *Mysticism after Modernity* I argued that mysticism should be seen, not as a special way of knowing, but simply as an embryonic form of radical theology. It was a kind of writing that was already trying to resolve the traditional ecclesiastical theology down into 'solar' or 'kingdom' religion. In particular, church religion sets up and insists on maintaining an unbridgeable gulf between Holy God and the sinful human being. The church's realistic view of God keeps believers in a state of permanent religious alienation and subjection, in order to terrify them into obedience and conformity. The mystical writer tries to deconstruct the gulf between God and the individual human being in order to overcome theological realism, unite the believer with God, and produce an effect of supreme happiness and liberation. It is of course because non-realist religion is such a wonderful release from realist religion that the church fears it, and has so often persecuted the mystics. For the church has always been a disciplinary organization that aims, not to fuse the divine and the human together, but to keep them apart for the sake of social control.

A third theme of recent years has been ontology, the theory of the nature of Being, or existence. In two books about 'Be-ing' I followed Heidegger in trying to overcome the traditional contrast between Eternal Being and temporal Becoming, saying that there is *only* temporal Be-ing. Be-ing is a continuous and gentle but very dense outpouring of pure contingency; a sort of white noise, which language differentiates and forms into the world of our experience. In my symbolism Be-ing is female, like 'the womb of time'.

The fourth of these new themes arrived in the three little 'Everyday Speech' books of 1999/2000, in which I tried to show that ordinary language is already 'the best radical theologian'. Study of the new idioms that have become established in the common language during the past half century or so shows the remarkable extent to which ordinary people have already demythologized God down into the contingent flux of life. The new 'Kingdom' form of religion is already taking shape. The reason why church Christianity is nowadays in such rapid decline is therefore not that it is being replaced by no religion, but that it is today being elbowed aside by its own fulfilment! It is to be noted that in the new globalized and communicative world, change is brought about not by the labours of individual geniuses, but by a shift in the general consensus of which we become aware only in retrospect.

These recent ideas converge to show how it is that religion today is fast becoming more democratic, more identified with the way ordinary people experience their life, and more ready to accept and embrace everything's transience. Belief in life after death is dying out. Religion is becoming less and less a matter of seeking an anchorage in a point somewhere outside life, and more and more a matter of simply saying Yes to life. In a final little trilogy I have tried to present my conclusions as *Philosophy's Own Religion* (2000), as a project for *Reforming Christianity* (2001), and as a synthesis of Eastern and Western thought in *Emptiness and Brightness* (2002). From now on I imagine that there will be some tidying-up operations, but the main thrust has been taken about as far as my abilities can take it.

And that is that. I am still sometimes asked to write an autobiography, but my writings have *been* my autobiography, in the sense that through them I have slowly worked my way towards a personal religious outlook and philosophy of life with which I can feel content. It has often been very hard going, but I am not complaining about anything. In my view, not only should one say Yes to life, but one should also in the end be able to say Amen to one's own life. That I hope I can do; and I shall be even more pleased if my own testimony proves to be of use to some other people.

15

JOHN ROBINSON AND THE LANGUAGE
OF FAITH IN GOD (2003)

My knowledge of John Robinson extended over a period of thirty years.
From 1952 to 1955 I was an undergraduate at Trinity Hall, Cambridge,
and frequently attended the Clare College Eucharist then presided over by
John with Bill Skelton and Charlie Moule. It embodied all the principles of
the Parish Communion Movement and was the best quality Christian worship available in Cambridge at that time. Of John's lectures in the Faculty
of Divinity I remember most vividly the course on *Romans* that was later
published. In March 1963, when *Honest to God* appeared, I had recently
succeeded John Habgood as Vice-Principal of Westcott House and was still
distinctly conservative in theology. Although I did sympathize strongly
with Robinson's motives in writing it, I was not deeply affected by his book.
But during the 1970s, when John had returned from Southwark to Trinity
College, I regularly attended a small dining club of theologians that met and
talked in his rooms, and in the early 1980s when my own extreme notoriety
began I was conscious of being shown much kindness by John. 'The Sixties
was my decade', he said to me, 'And the Eighties will be yours'—which
shows that Eric James was right to say in his biography that John loved the
limelight, and had greatly enjoyed the huge publicity that surrounded him
during 'his' decade.[1]

* * * *

As I have said, I was not at first impressed by *Honest to God*. It seemed
to be surprisingly clumsily written and obscure, and Robinson's use of the
word 'God' seemed to be all over the place. He handed with confidence
the Bible's mythical realism about God—the God enthroned 'up there' who
is described in the language of worship—but he seemed rather ill-at-ease
with classical Christian theism, as Herbert McCabe showed in an acute
review.[2] This was odd, and at the time we put it down to the fact that John
was a New Testament scholar and not a philosopher. We supposed that, like
Rudolf Bultmann, he was jumping straight from the biblical world-view to
the modern world-view, and neglecting the extent to which the long doctrinal and philosophical development in between had sought, and sometimes
found, ways of bridging the gap. In those days of the 1950s and early 1960s
there were still some formidable neo-Thomists and other exponents of classical Christian theism around. Such people's God-talk was confident and
orderly enough to create a climate in which it was very possible for readers
to be dismissive about *Honest to God*.

Fifteen or twenty years later, however, some of us began to see the issues very differently. In the years immediately after the Second World War figures like St Thomas Aquinas and Karl Marx, Freud and Sartre had seemed to dominate the intellectual landscape. The issues of the day were debated under labels such as Catholicism, communism and secular humanism; logical positivism and existentialism; and theism, agnosticism and atheism. Now, all these names and 'positions' began to fade away, to be replaced by new names and a new agenda. Instead of talking about the clash between Catholicism and communism, we began to talk about the end of metaphysics, the Death of God and the emergence of postmodernity. And the presiding genius of the new age was Friedrich Nietzsche. At some date in the Seventies or Eighties you had to give yourself a crash course in Nietzsche: mine, I vividly remember, took place in the first half of 1981.

Amongst the radical theologians of the 1960s there were at least two—the Americans, Thomas J. J. Altizer and William Hamilton[3]—who had been fully aware of the importance of Nietzsche for modern theology. Their nearest counterparts in Britain were Werner and Lotte Pelz;[4] but these were, alas, rather marginal figures, and for many years Nietzsche had seemed to us too excessive and fearsome a writer to be approachable.

Gradually, however, during the late 1970s, people in Britain were beginning to wonder how far the leading thinkers of the twentieth century had all along been aware of Nietzsche and had recognized the significance of his work. The answer came as a surprise: word had indeed gone round, and during their youth many or most of the major thinkers of the German-speaking world had put in a period of study at the Nietzsche-Archive. After about 1900 the leading younger Germans somehow just knew that Nietzsche was canonical. He was someone you lived 'after', and therefore someone you had to have assimilated—*in full*. His work had made everything different, but because of his popular reputation many people drew a discreet veil over the extent of their personal debt to him. Something like this was true of thinkers as various as Freud and Jung, Heidegger and Gadamer, Thomas Mann and (amongst the theologians) at least of Albert Schweitzer, Paul Tillich, Bultmann and Bonhoeffer.

You will have noticed that the three post-Nietzschean theologians just mentioned are the very ones whose work Robinson was interpreting in *Honest to God*. And that leads me to the second point on which our view of *Honest to God* changed after 1980: belatedly, we began to realise that John Robinson was not quite as unphilosophical as we had supposed. In fact, like Albert Schweitzer, he had written his Ph.D. Dissertation, *not* on a New Testament topic, but on a topic in the philosophy of religion. Schweitzer's topic was Kant's Philosophy of Religion—which helps us to grasp that for the rest of his life Schweitzer, following Kant, took a non-realist view of

God: for him, God was just Love, a guiding spiritual ideal. Robinson's topic was Martin Buber's personalist philosophy of religion, which at that time was very influential amongst theologians. Like the others we have mentioned, Buber was concerned about the reconstruction of religious thought after Nietzsche, and two of his doctrines are highly relevant to our present topic.[5] First, Buber made a sharp distinction between two different ways in which we may relate ourselves to whatever we are dealing with: we may treat it as impersonal, or we may respond to and address it as utterly personal. Buber called these two attitudes *I-It* and *I-Thou*. Then secondly, Buber also said that we could take up the *I-Thou* attitude to Everything, at cosmic level, recognized as an Eternal Thou. In such a case, according to Buber, we just *intuit* the personal: its call and our response may be unmediated by anything empirical. The eternal Thou, it was said, calls us, and can be addressed by us, but can never be described. It is always and only our Lord. We know it only as a claim upon us.

These doctrines seemed in their heyday to offer theology a vocabulary in which one could continue to talk about God, about the ultimacy of personal values, about God's self-revelation, and about personal relations between humans and God, after Nietzsche, after the end of metaphysics, and even after the end of 'realistic' or literal belief in miracles.

Such were the ideas that John Robinson adopted. They were quite common amongst the 'dialectical theologians' and the 'theologians of encounter' who were much read in the years just before and after the Second World War, and they are very prominent in *Honest to God*. Robinson's biggest success was amongst the armies of people who flourished in the Welfare State's 'helping professions'—teachers, counsellors, therapists, health visitors, district nurses, social workers, probation officers and so on. These people were a new clergy, and their work was a new version of the pastoral work that in the past had been done by the parish priest and his wife. They were (roughly) post-Christian religious humanists, who were very ready to hear that to believe in God was to believe in the ultimacy of the personal, of personal values and personal relations. Personalism was *exactly* their worldview, and it was their enthusiasm for his book that buoyed Robinson up so much in the 1960s, during the years immediately following the publication of *Honest to God*.

All this is I hope sufficient to explain how and why our view of John Robinson's work changed around 1980 or so. The first decades after the War had been dominated by Freud and Marx, by secular humanism and socialism. Society was being reconstructed after the War, and the new professions were helping people to settle in and adjust to the welfare state, consumerism and the media society. In that context, the public naturally tended to see *Honest to God* as a work of ultra-liberal theology that cut out the supernatural and translated theological statements into statements about human relationships. The religious was the 'depth' of the interpersonal. But by the 1980s the culture had changed, and we began to see Robinson in a new way. In the manner of the Germans he admired—Tillich, Bultmann and Bonhoeffer—Robinson was trying to find a new use for God-language and a future for religious thought *after* Nietzsche and the Death of God. Society was becoming so mobile and democratic that all objective norms and realities were crumbling. This was more than just secular humanism: it was something like nihilism.

Robinson was not, as rightwingers alleged, a crazed reductionist, throwing the faith to the wolves of secularism piece by piece: *Honest to God* was his *normal* theology, and its aim was constructive. He was not discarding, he was rebuilding; and he repeatedly warns his readers that the twentieth-century crisis of faith is much graver than they yet realise. From Michael Ramsey downwards, the conservatives declared that 'John Robinson went too far', and he of course replied that posterity would probably judge that he had not gone nearly far enough. And he was obviously right.

There was however a persistent ambiguity in the message of *Honest to God*. In the end, was the book teaching a realist view of God and god-language—or was it teaching non-realism? It's hard to say, because some of Robinson's statements and arguments clearly imply a non-realist view of God, whereas in other places Robinson uses realist language that equally clearly asserts that God exists independently of human faith in him. Which was Robinson's view? It is very hard to say, because most of twentieth-century German Protestant theology—including Tillich, Bultmann and Bonhoeffer—was itself highly ambiguous on this point, because it *had* to be so, and Robinson seems to want to shelter behind that ambiguity.

I take these three points in turn. First, then, as the philosopher Alasdair MacIntyre pointed out, many of John Robinson's arguments were clearly arguments for non-realism. Unfortunately MacIntyre confuses non-realism with atheism, a mistake that continues to be common to this day, but the main point is clear enough:

> [Dr. Robinson] is prepared to translate theological statements into non-theological. He says that what we mean when we speak of God is 'that which concerns us ultimately'; that to speak of God is to speak of the deepest things we experience. 'Belief in God is a matter of "what you take seriously without any reservation"', and to assert that God is love is to assert the supremacy of personal relationships. All theological statements can consequently be translated into statements about human concern.[6]

Here MacIntyre is making a general point about modern Protestant theology. If you give up metaphysics, if you give up the attempt to prove the objective existence of God, then all you are left with is the 'my god' of personal religion. And the 'my god' is non-realist. He is internal to us: 'my god' is my goal in life, my spiritual ideal that I am trying to live up to, my dream, my hope. God becomes a function of human religiousness: not a being out there, but rather the ideal towards which my faith orients me, the imaginary focus of my own spiritual project. And because MacIntyre assumes that everyone who is not a realist must be an atheist, he deduces that Robinson is an atheist.

Now it is certainly arguable that ever since Luther, Protestant faith has been of this kind—a personal religious project, oriented towards an ideal God. And it is also arguable that today, when our philosophy and our science no longer require an objectively-real God out there, all of Christian faith is and has to be of the non-realist type. The word 'God' still does a job in religion, but it no longer explains events all over the place in the way it did. But as I know and you know, the Churches certainly are not prepared to endorse a non-realist reading of their own faith, and John Robinson wasn't prepared to accept it either. Both in *Honest to God* and in all the subsequent debate he continued to affirm the reality of God, speaking for example of God's as 'an other reality', of 'ultimate reality as gracious', of 'the reality of Being as gracious', and so on.[7] It seems that God's reality is not limited to the sphere of human subjective religiosity, but is objective.

However, although Robinson does want to speak of the reality of God, he also says that he is not to be understood as attempting to reinstate the old God, the God of the philosophers. For Robinson's God doesn't *do* anything: he is not causally active. The best-remembered illustration of this is the fact that in 1983, after his cancer was diagnosed, Robinson regularly declared that he did not think of God as having *caused* the cancer, but he did believe that God could be found *in* the cancer.[8]

What did this mean? Robinson declared that God is an inescapable 'reality of life'. In all the circumstances of life, without exception, he said that he 'found himself' held in the same 'utterly personal' relationship of claim and grace. So he fell back on Buber's intuition of an eternal Thou. He calls it 'real', but he cannot spell out its reality in any way that might make sense to a philosopher.

So the ambiguity remains to the end. Robinson would (I think) have continued to claim to be a theological realist to the end of his life—without ever openly disagreeing with me—and in reply to him I would say that unless he can do something to restore metaphysics, his view doesn't and cannot differ from my own non-realism—the point being, of course, that the notion of objective 'reality' is highly metaphysical. So as I see it, the ambiguity remains and runs through all of John Robinson's work, as it runs through most of twentieth-century theology. It has some troubling consequences.

One is that today's language about God very often sounds confused and unclear. For example, sometimes people talk as if the reality of God is objective and constraining, but at other times people talk as if they are aware that *they themselves* have made a moral decision about what sort of God they are going to be ready to believe in. Such talk is obvious non-realism. Sometimes people talk as if *God* gives them strength and comfort in adversity, but at other times they say that it is *their own faith* from which they derive comfort. The prophet Elijah would say to that: 'How long will you go limping with two different opinions?'[9] And he might make the same remark about the well-known and freely-admitted fact that church leaders nowadays have two faiths. There is the common ecclesiastical faith to which they are institutionally committed by their office, and which they must unhesitatingly defend in public; and there is the personal faith to which they have been led by their own study and thinking. Every church leader who is theologically educated is aware of the gap between the two, and of the devices that must be used to conceal it.

John Robinson was aware of difficulties like these: they were pressed upon him by his critics. But twentieth-century theology was not able to resolve them, and Robinson himself within four years or so (that is, by 1967) had gone as far as he could with them. Perhaps the twenty-first century will do better. We see the issues a little more clearly now than they did in the 1960s, and we see very much more clearly how late the hour is and how urgent the question of reform and renewal has become.

16

SUMMARIES

Most of the great religions have produced short mnemonic formulae which are used in teaching catechumens. The Buddhist ones—the Four Noble Truths, the Three Jewels, the Eightfold Path and so on—are particularly good. I have often tried to compose such summaries myself, because people always seem to find my ideas very obscure and difficult, and I want to achieve as much simplicity and clarity as I can. So here are some examples of the many summaries that I have composed and distributed to lecture audiences as handouts during the past ten years or so. When I look again at them, I see that some of them are not so much short sketches of my own teachings as rather descriptions of the background out of which my ideas have arisen and against which they will, as I hope, make sense.

The summaries are classified under three headings: philosophy, philosophy's approach to religion, and various reformulations of Christianity.

PHILOSOPHY

A. Where We Are Now: A Democratic Philosophy of Life

1. Until about two centuries ago human life was seen as being lived on a fixed stage, and as ruled by eternal norms of truth and value. (The old world picture may nowadays be called 'realism', 'platonism' or 'metaphysics.')
2. But now everything is contingent: that is, humanly-postulated, mediated by language and historically-evolving. There is nothing but the flux.
3. There is no Eternal Order of Reason above us that fixes all meanings and truths and values. Language is unanchored.
4. Modern society then no longer has any overarching and authoritative myth. Modern people are 'homeless' and feel threatened by nihilism.
5. We no longer have any ready-made or 'dogmatic' truth and we have no access to any 'certainties' or 'absolutes' that exist independently of us.
6. We are, and we have to be, democrats and pragmatists who must go along with a current-consensus world view.
7. Our firmest ground and starting-point is the vocabulary and world view of ordinary language and everyday life, as expressed for example in such typically modern media as the novel and the newspaper.
8. The special vocabularies and world-views of science and religion should be seen as extensions or supplements built out of the life-world, and checked back against it.

9. Science furthers the purposes of life by differentiating the life-world, developing causal theories, establishing mathematical relationships and inventing technologies.

10. Religion seeks to overcome nihilism, and give value to life. In religion we seek to develop shared meanings, purposes, narratives. Religion's last concern is with eternal happiness in the face of death.

Written as a handout for a public lecture in Newcastle-on-Tyne in about 1997, and subsequently published in the Sea of Faith Magazine *No. 32, Spring 1998.*

B. The Six Truths

1. ALL THIS IS OUTSIDELESS. Radical immanence. There is nothing hidden. What you see is what there is.

2. IT ALL JUST HAPPENS THIS WAY. Radical contingency. Nothing founds or finalizes; everything is just customarily associated.

3. MEANING COMES FIRST. Culturalism, the (logical) priority of culture. Our evolving sign-systems, theories etc. shape our world.

4. EVERYTHING IS PUBLIC. There is no metaphysical core-self or privileged inner citadel. Subjectivity and the inner life are *also* cultural products.

5. EVERYTHING IS HISTORICAL, developing by the interplay of forces in the public realm. We are evolving all the rules and all the meanings.

6. NOTHING SAYS IT MUST ALL ADD UP. Nothing's laid on; there is no guarantee of systematic coherence, nor of the victory of the good.

Transcribed from a lecture handout written for a day conference in Christchurch, New Zealand, in 1991. Used again as the basis for chapter 3 of The Time Being *(London: SCM Press, 1993). For a more elaborate summary of my philosophy, see* The Last Philosophy *(London: SCM Press, 1995), pp. 117–20.*

THE WAY IN TO RELIGIOUS THINKING

A. Post-dogmatic Religion

1. There is no specially-privileged right vocabulary.

2. There is no divinely approved right 'angle', or order of exposition.

3. There is no One, True and Final system of religious doctrine, God's own story about himself, told just as he wants it to be told.

4. Religious teaching in the future cannot be framed as merely a simplified and liberalized version of the scripture-and-doctrine-based reli-

gion we have known hitherto. On the contrary, religious teaching must not ever again be allowed to become codified, fixed and sacrosanct. On the contrary, it must have the all-round corrigibility that is the mark of every modern system of knowledge.

5. In religion, ethics and the philosophy of life the price of truth from now on is constant self-criticism and the readiness to remint all one's metaphors.

6. It follows from all this that second-hand belief in creeds drawn up by other people in the past, and handed down to us, is now of no religious value whatever. The only religious beliefs that avail are ones that we have framed ourselves, or found in ourselves, and have checked out in life and in conversation with others.

7. The religion of the future, then, will be a pilgrim religion that we ourselves are consciously making and remaking all the time. We will be like artists, permanent pilgrims with no fixed abode, improvising our own spiritualities and our own life-stories as we go along. Indeed, this is how most of us already are.

From The Way to Happiness, *ms. version, pp. 39f.*

B. True Religion Is Your Own Voice

1. In religion, as in other subjects, *we should not accept any beliefs dogmatically*. No belief should be accepted because it is traditional, or because it is greatly venerated. In fact, we should not accept *any* second-hand or ready-made religious convictions.

2. Religious truth is of a kind that has to be personally appropriated, and tested out ethically in one's own life. Hence the relevant test-procedure differs somewhat from the ones used in science and history. The rule is that *the only true religious beliefs for you will be beliefs that you personally have appropriated and tested out in your own life, and have articulated and defended in conversation with others.*

3. (Corollary of 2): From this it is clear that *the only true religious beliefs are heresies*, i.e. beliefs that one has chosen for oneself and made one's own, item by item. All orthodoxies, being presented to us for acceptance *en bloc* and ready-made, must be rejected. Besides, when did Tradition ever actually turn out to be right about anything at all?

4. For you, *true religion is your own voice*—a personal faith that you have evolved over a period of many years, and have checked out rigorously in your living, and in your conversation with your own generation.

From ibid., p. 86.

REINTERPRETING CHRISTIANITY

A. Sea of Faith Theology

1. God is the religious ideal—a unifying symbol of our common values, and of the goal of the religious life.
2. The God of Christians is love: i.e. the Christian specification of the religious ideal makes Love the highest value.
3. The ideal of love is embodied in human form in Jesus of Nazareth, the stories about him, and the institutions etc. that have grown around him.

This was first written about 1991 for a Cambridge undergraduate audience, and is quoted in After God *(New York: Harper Collins Basic Books and London: Weidenfeld and Nicholson, 1997), pp. 127f. The version cited was written for a lecture in Guildford Cathedral in, I think, the year 2001.*

B. The Non-realist Interpretation of Christian Doctrine

Doctrine	Realist interpretation	Non-realist interpretation
Creation	God as First Cause of the world; God causes the Big Bang . . .	Life should be treated as a pure gift (Bultmann).
Providence	God pre-ordains and supervises the entire course of world-events, and of each life.	I believe I will come through: my faith will not let me down (Tillich, S. F.).
Prayer	One seeks favours from a Godfather, or petitions a great King. The place of worship is a 'basilica', a royal audience-hall.	Intercessory prayer as an expression of love and concern, and a way of *supporting* the one prayed for. Prayer as attention to be-ing.
Incarnation	The metaphysical Son of God takes a human life as his own, and becomes its subject.	Jesus is seen as embodying the religious ideal; he is Love in human form.
Resurrection	Jesus rises bodily from the Tomb.	The believer who identifies himself with Jesus and dies with him in baptism rises to live a new, risen life.
Ascension	Jesus goes bodily up to a local Heaven in the sky.	The believer salutes Jesus as 'Lord' in his life (St Paul, Romans).
Eternal life	Post-mortem life in Heaven.	The 'solar' living of the believer, who is no longer afraid of death.

First written for a seminar at Perth, WA, in October 2002, and then rewritten for a student audience at Canterbury Christ Church University College, in the Spring of 2003. The Tillich allusion is to a book called The Shaking of the Foundations.

C. A Very Short Summary of My Views
Energetic Spinozism, poetical theology, solar ethics.

This formulation is quoted in several of my books of the late Nineties. I admired John Mackie's summary of philosophy: 'fallible knowledge and invented ethics', and wanted to produce something equally crisp. See Solar Ethics *(London: SCM Press, 1995), p. 1, and the paper 'Post-Christianity', in Paul Heelas, ed.,* Religion, Modernity and Post-Modernity *(Malden, MAM and Oxford, Blackwell, 1998).*

D. Redefining Religion
1. *The whole of life is religious.* This is a consequence of 'the erasure of the distinction between the sacred and the profane'.
2. *Transient ourselves, we should commit ourselves unreservedly to our own transient lives.* There is nothing that threatens to rob us of either the meanings of the words we use or the values by which we live. Nor do we ever step outside life.
3. *We should pursue salvation, not by an ascetical withdrawal from the world, but by expressive living.*
4. *Life and death are not polar opposites, and neither is ever experienced 'pure'.*
5. *The last stage in the historical evolution of religion is . . . universal religious humanism and the last ethic is humanitarian.*
6. *We no longer require any great narrative scheme of doctrine: the old systematic theology should be replaced by storytelling about the religious significance of our own time and the history that has brought us to it.*
7. *For the sake of our spiritual integrity, it is best for the present not to insist too much upon the merely local and 'positive' features of religion. . . . There is no great and unique religious object, but we can appropriately take up religious attitudes towards bare prelinguistic Be-ing, towards the whole fountain of actual Being, and towards the brightness of everything.*

From Philosophy's Own Religion *(London: SCM Press, 2000), the conclusions to each of the sections in Part Three, pp. 136–67.*

17

ENVOI

To understand what makes the radical theologian tick, one must understand the dispensationalist view of history which is deeply engrained in the Bible, and therefore in both the Jewish and the Christian traditions—and also in such later offshoots from them as Marxist communism and liberalism. Dispensationalism sees the whole of human history as a great drama of fall and redemption, bondage and liberation, unfolding in several acts. Each act in the drama is a distinct divinely-ordained dispensation, during which human life is lived under a particular set of conditions. For example, in the Biblical and Latin Christian scheme the Age of the Patriarchs, the Age of the Mosaic Law, and the Age of the Church are three distinct dispensations. Each has its own theology, its own established religious system and channels of grace, and its own moral order. The transition between one dispensation and the next is usually seen as catastrophic, or as involving a death and rebirth: the old order decays, and people feel the birth-pangs of the new age as it struggles to be born.

Two points in this account so far deserve special emphasis. *First*, the old 'orthodox' Christianity was thoroughly dispensationalist, and dispensationalists cannot regard either dogma, or the religious system, or the current moral code as being timeless 'absolutes'. On the contrary, they are all of them relative to the dispensation under which one is living. The old theologians noticed, for example, that in the Age of the Patriarchs it had apparently been morally lawful for a great man of God to keep several wives and a small army of concubines, and that at the time of the Exodus it was morally lawful for the Israelites to 'spoil' (i.e., cheat) the Egyptians. Similarly, the old theologians noticed that at one time the right way to approach God was by animal sacrifice; but now things are different. And again, the leading Christian doctrines—the Incarnation and the Trinity—are strongly dispensational. Thus, whatever else we may want to say about it, the old dispensationalist world-view carried with it at least an implicit recognition of the historical relativity of religious truth and religious law. Today's neo-conservatives, with their talk of 'absolutes' and their denunciation of 'relativism', have not yet thought about the tradition to which they appeal so confidently.

Secondly, it has in all ages been common for people to think that the next major transition, scheduled to come at the end of the present world-age (or saeculum, or dispensation), is going to be especially violent. In Marxist terms, it is 'the Revolution'; in popular Christian terms it will be the End of the World, the Second Coming of Christ, and the establishment on earth of his millennial kingdom. The coming new dispensation may also be called the Messianic Age, or the Kingdom of God on earth, or the Sabbath Rest of the Saints. It will be marked by a general resurrection of 'the saints', who are all those Christians who have lived in the hope of seeing Christ's return, but who died while still waiting.

So, like other revolutionaries, Christians have lived in the ardent hope of seeing the end of the present (unsatisfactory) dispensation, and the coming of a new and better world in the way that is rather hazily described in the last pages of the New Testament.

Even as late as the mid-nineteenth century, a poet like Alfred Tennyson could still end his masterpiece by invoking that 'one far-off divine event / To which the whole creation moves'.[1] Why has it been so long delayed? Can anything be done to speed it?

Yes! In their various ways ascetics, mystics and theologians may express, in their deeds and in their writings, an urgent yearning to see the new world, and an impatient attempt to burst out of the constraints of the present world order. In their different ways, the monk and the mystic have tried to anticipate—that is, to seize and to live in advance—the life of the new world. They are, as it were, deliberately jumping the gun: they are trying to push God into acting. From the old 'realist' point of view it sounds rather presumptuous to do such a thing: but from the 'non-realist' point of view it makes good sense. After all it always *was* we humans who by our own cultural and religious development keep pushing the story on another chapter. The radical theologian is not really trying to push *God* into acting, but he *is* trying to push his fellow-Christians into actually building the world they profess to hope for.

An attempt in this way to force the pace of history has become very familiar to us in modern times in its political form. The revolutionary and the terrorist are very often trying to provoke the Last Battle at the end of the age, in the belief that they can thus speed the victory of their cause.[2] Very similarly, extreme ascetics like the Qumran Community which wrote the Dead Sea Scrolls are struggling to accelerate the end of history and the final triumph of God. The idea is to put yourself into a state of such distress that God will feel that he must not delay your vindication any longer.

Elsewhere I have argued that the typical mystic is another terrorist of the spirit. She longs for union with God, but knows very well that deification is heresy during the present dispensation. The ontological difference between God and the human soul cannot be fully overcome. Nevertheless, the mystic strains against and struggles to subvert the religious limits under which we must presently live. Often, she'll announce that she has achieved the impossible, full union with God. Then she will be burnt alive for her pains; for when she is understood, she must of course be condemned.[3]

In all this, the classical ascetics and mystics were forerunners of the radical theologian, whose message is always the same: 'It's about time we pushed the Christian movement forwards, to the next stage of its long-foreseen development.' That means moving forward from ecclesiastical Christianity to the more Quakerish, post-ecclesiastical, 'kingdom' type of religion that Jesus originally demanded.[4] For two thousand years we have been postponing implementation of his programme, claiming that the world isn't yet ready for it. But during the twentieth century we at last reached humanitarian liberal democracy, and the enfranchisement of both sexes and all races. Surely we *have* now come to—or at least, we are getting close to—the kind of free, universal, and multi-ethnic society that our tradition always hoped to see at the end of history? In which case we have come to what the old supernatural doctrine thought of as 'the return of Christ'—namely, a world in which we can at last live in the way Jesus originally demanded, and practise the post-institutional, immediate kind of religion that he taught. It seems we've come full circle, and are back to the point at which it all began. Now we can really begin to *live*, now and in this present world!

So I have been saying for a few years now; but I haven't a chance, for reasons that Fyodor Dostoyevsky stated very clearly in *The Brothers Karamazov*.[5] The Church has been deferring Jesus for 2000 years. The apparatus by which it defers the practice of his immediate kind of religion has grown to be so big and elaborate that it has by now totally obscured that which it defers. The results has been that everyone now equates Christianity with the apparatus by means of which the Church *defers* Christianity, and this has all become so deeply engrained that I have hardly a chance of being heard and understood.

At this point it is necessary to make clear that, at least on my account of radical theology, there is no distinctive essence of Christianity. *The apparatus by means of which the Church defers Christianity*—that is, the Scriptures, the creeds, the church, the ministry and the sacraments and so on—is packaged in a distinctive vocabulary, and comes with many supporting certificates, guarantees and trademarks. It can therefore easily be thought of as being *itself* distinctively Christian. But the ethical substance of Christianity, the way of engaging with life and the kind of social world that ever since biblical times we have always hoped to see, has nothing distinctively Christian about it. It's what we *all of us* want, 'philosophy's own religion', life really lived to the full. It's no more than what Martin Luther King and John Lennon were talking about only a few decades ago. The 'distinctively-Christian' branding, whether of the Catholic, or Orthodox, or reformed Evangelical protestant type, does not brand the true religion: its function is merely to boost the authority of one particular priesthood. No more than that: in the end we can and we should forget it.

All this makes clear why the whole subject of success and failure in one's project is so ambiguous for a radical theologian. He is in the same sort of position as the prophet Jonah. Jonah, it will be remembered, prophesied doom unless Nineveh repented. Nineveh heard him, and duly repented. Doom was averted, and Jonah was angry. He had *succeeded* in his prophetic mission, but *his prophecy had failed*, and he felt frustrated and angry, and wanted to die. He couldn't escape the paradox that his success had left him a failed prophet who looked like a fool. And the radical theologian is not much better off, for his message is such that the church must flatly reject it. If he succeeds in getting the message across, he surely *must* be thrown out.

Perhaps I should conclude that there is after all something distinctive about the biblical and Judaeo-Christian tradition, namely the way in which in it success and failure are always intertwined. You do your best—and you are an unprofitable servant. You strive with all your might—in the knowledge that all our striving is but a jest. And you do not complain.

NOTES

Introduction

1. Alan Ryan, *J. S. Mill*, p. 3.

2. According to their own testimony, this is especially true of episcopal radicals such as Victor Pike, John S. Spong and Richard Holloway.

3. See for example my *Kingdom Come in Everyday Speech*.

4. Dorothée Sölle, whose death occurred in early 2003, was perhaps the best-known female radical theologian to date. Other radical women have usually preferred to fight under the banner of feminist theology.

5. See my *The Meaning of It All in Everyday Speech*. The argument in the remaining pages of this essay is developed further in *Life, Life* and in *The Way to Happiness*.

Chapter 10

1. *First and Last Things*, pp. 70ff.

2. Aylmer Maude, *Life of Tolstoy*, p. 51. For Kant, see *Religion within the Limits of Reason Alone*, pp. 54–60.

3. R. A. Nicholson, *Rümï*, p. 44. 'Ibnu'l-'Arabi (1165–1240) was an Andalusian, and the principal systematic thinker of Sufism. Jalalu'l-Dïn Rümï (1207–73) was a Persian, and founder of the Mevlevi Order.

4. *Christ and the Hiddenness of God*, pp. 138–67. For an authoritative recent discussion of the resurrection, see C. F. Evans, *Resurrection and the New Testament*.

Chapter 11

1. John Hunt, *Religious Thought in England*, vol. III, p. 124.

2. *Revelation and Religion*, pp. 195–96.

3. E.g. Mark 10.18, Luke 12.14, Mark 13.32, etc.

Chapter 12

1. In the Introduction to the Everyman edition of Renan's *Life of Jesus*, p. xvii.

2. Charles Gore, *Incarnation of the Son of God*, p. 143.

3. H. P. Liddon, *Divinity of our Lord*, pp. 153ff.

4. *Divinity of our Lord*, p. 472.

5. Gore, *Dissertations*, pp. 162ff.

6. Liddon, *Divinity of our Lord*, pp. 164, 168, xxxvi, 175.

7. For what follows see N. H. Baynes, *Byzantine Studies*, especially VII, IX and XV.

8. *Byzantine Studies*, IX.

9. T. Klauser, *Short History*, pp. 32–37.

10. See Eta Linnemann, *Parables of Jesus*.

11. E.g. John Beckwith, *Early Christian and Byzantine Art*, plates 176, 222, 256, 292.

12. E.g. Hans von Campenhausen, *Tradition and Life*, p. 190. Notice too how in the late medieval West, God the Father was commonly portrayed as the Pope, wearing the Triple Crown, as in well-known works by Van Eyck and Boticelli.

13. A. Grillmeier has studied this question: for example, *Der Logos am Kreuz*.

14. Klauser, *Short History*, pp. 30ff. and notes. See especially A. Jungmann, *The Place of Christ in Liturgical Prayer*.

15. This original doctrinal basis agreed in 1938 was later, in 1961, exchanged for a trinitarian one.

16. F. Van der Meer and Christine Mohrmann, *Atlas of the Early Christian World*, illustration 321 (Palestine c. 600); Beckwith, *Early Christian and Byzantine Art*, plate 118.

17. Images of the Trinity as three *similar* men go back as far as the 'Dogmatic Sarcophagus' in the Lateran Museum (c. 330).

18. Brief account in H. Skrobucha, *Icons*, pp. 17f. In this section I acknowledge with grateful thanks the help of the Warburg Institute and the courtesy of its librarian.

19. Francis Wormald, *English Drawings*, plates 4(a), 4(b), 5(a). But see Pembroke College Cambridge, MS120, pi. 6, upper half, for what appears to be an early English Paternity.

20. A good example is the Father's head emerging from the cloud at Christ's baptism, on the font at S. Bartelemy, Liege, by Renier de Huy, 1111–18. And see F. E. Hulme, *Symbolism in Christian Art*, pp. 43ff.; Margaret Rickert, *Painting in Britain*, plates 92, 102, 178; and W. Braunfels, *Die Heilige Dreifaltigkeit*.

21. A reproduction of this bizarre work, and scholarly material about it, are to be found in the collections of the Warburg Institute, mentioned above in n.18.

22. Austin Farrer, *Said or Sung*, pp. 116ff.

23. Wittgenstein, *Lectures and Conversations*, p. 63.

Chapter 15

1. See Eric James, *A Life of Bishop John A. T. Robinson,*.

2. Reprinted in John A. T. Robinson and D. L. Edwards, *The Honest to God Debate*, pp. 165–80.

3. T. J. J. Altizer and W. Hamilton, *Radical Theology and the Death of God*.

4. Werner and Lotte Pelz, *God Is No More*.

5. Martin Buber, *I and Thou*.

6. *The Honest to God Debate*, p. 215.

7. For these phrases see especially the lecture 'Can a Truly Contemporary Person *Not* Be an Atheist?' reprinted in John A. T. Robinson, *The New Reformation?*, pp. 106–22.

8. John A. T. Robinson, *Where Three Ways Meet*, p. 190.

9. I Kings 18:21 (RSV).

Chapter 17

1. *In Memoriam A. H. H.*, Epilogue, ll.143f.

2. These points are made very well by Jean Baudrillard in his philosophy of history—for example in the essay: "The Year 2000 Will Not Take Place," pp. 23–25.

3. *Mysticism After Modernity*.

4. *Reforming Christianity*.

5. Book 5, chapter 5, 'The Grand Inquisitor'.

BIBLIOGRAPHY

T. J. J. Altizer and W. Hamilton, *Radical Theology and the Death of God.* Harmondsworth: Penguin Books, 1968.

Jean Baudrillard, "The Year 2000 Will Not Take Place." Pp. 18–28 in *FUTUR*FALL: Excursions into Post-Modernity.* Edited by E.A. Grosz et al. Sydney: Power Institute of Fine Arts, 1988.

N. H. Baynes, *Byzantine Studies and Other Essays.* London: Athlone Press, 1955.

John Beckwith, *Early Christian and Byzantine Art.* Harmondsworth: Penguin Books, 1970.

W. Braunfels, *Die Heilige Dreifaltigkeit.* Dusseldorf, 1954.

Martin Buber, *I and Thou,* Translated by R. Gregor Smith. Edinburgh: T. & T. Clark, 1937.

Hans von Campenhausen, *Tradition and Life in the Church: essays and lectures in Church history.* Translated by A. V. Littledale. London: Collins, 1968.

Don Cupitt, *Christ and the Hiddenness of God.* London: Lutterworth Press, 1971.

———, *Kingdom Come in Everyday Speech.* London: SCM Press, 2000.

———, *Life, Life.* Santa Rosa, CA: Polebridge Press, 2003.

———, *The Meaning of It All in Everyday Speech.* London: SCM Press, 1999.

———, *Mysticism after Modernity.* Malden, MA, & Oxford: Blackwell Publishers, 1998.

———, *Reforming Christianity.* Santa Rosa, CA: Polebridge Press, 2001.

———, *The Way to Happiness: A Theory of Religion.* Santa Rosa, CA: Polebridge Press, 2005.

C. F. Evans, *Resurrection and the New Testament.* London: SCM Press, 1970.

H. H. Farmer, *Revelation and Religion.* London: Nisbet & Co., 1954.

Austin Farrer, *Said or Sung. An arrangement of homily and verse.* London: Faith Press, 1960.

Charles Gore, *Dissertations on Subjects Connected with the Incarnation.* London: John Murray, 1895.

———, *The Incarnation of the Son of God, being the Bampton Lectures for the year 1891.* London: John Murray, 1891.

A. Grillmeier, *Der Logos am Kreuz.* Munich, 1956.

F. E. Hulme, *Symbolism in Christian Art.* Revised and illustrated edition. Poole: Blandford Press, 1976.

John Hunt, *Religious Thought in England.* Vol. III. London: Strahan, 1870–1873.

Eric James, *A Life of Bishop John A. T. Robinson, Scholar, Pastor, Prophet.* London: Collins, 1987.

A. Jungmann, *The Place of Christ in Liturgical Prayer.* 2nd revised edition. Translated by A. Peeler. London & Dublin: Geoffrey Chapman, 1965.

Immanuel Kant, *Religion within the Limits of Reason Alone.* Translated with an introduction and notes by Theodore M. Greene and Hoyt H. Hudson. Harper Torchbooks. New York: Harper & Bros., 1960.

T. Klauser, *A Short History of the Western Liturgy: an account and some reflections.*
    Translated from the German by John Halliburton. London: Oxford University
    Press, 1969.
H. P. Liddon, *The Divinity of our Lord and Saviour Jesus Christ: eight lectures
    preached before the University of Oxford in 1866, on the foundation of the late
    Rev. John Bampton.* Fourteenth edition. London: Longmans, 1890.
Eta Linnemann, *Parables of Jesus, introduction and exposition.* Translated by John
    Sturdy. London: SPCK, 1966.
Aylmer Maude, *The Life of Tolstoy: Later Years.* World's Classics edition. London:
    Oxford University Press, 1930.
F. Van der Meer and Christine Mohrmann, *Atlas of the Early Christian World.*
    Translated and edited by Mary F. Hedlund and H.H. Rowley. London: Thomas
    Nelson & Sons, 1958.
R. A. Nicholson, *Rümï, poet and mystic, 1207–1273: selections from his writings.*
    Translated with introduction and notes by Reynold A. Nicholson. London:
    George Allen & Unwin, 1950.
Werner Pelze and Lotte Pelz, *God Is No More.* London: Victor Gollancz, 1963.
Ernest Renan, *Life of Jesus.* Everyman's Library. London: Dent, [1927].
Margaret Rickert, *Painting in Britain: the Middle Ages.* London: Penguin Books,
    1954.
John A.T. Robinson, *The New Reformation?* London: SCM Press, 1965.
_____, *Where Three Ways Meet: Last Essays and Sermons.* London: SCM Press,
    1987.
John A. T. Robinson and D. L. Edwards, *The Honest to God Debate.* London: SCM
    Press, 1963.
Alan Ryan, *J.S. Mill.* London & Boston: Routledge & Kegan Paul, 1974.
H. Skrobucha, *Icons.* Translated by M. v. Herzfeld and R. Gaze. Edinburgh &
    London: Oliver & Boyd, 1963.
H. G. Wells, *First and Last Things.* London : Watts & Co, 1929 (1930).
Ludwig Wittgenstein, *Lectures and Conversations on aesthetics, psychology and reli-
    gious belief.* Edited by Cyril Barrett. London: Blackwell, 1966.
Francis Wormald, English Drawings of the Tenth and Eleventh Centuries, London:
    Faber & Faber, 1952.

INDEX

This book is a collection, and some of the work of an indexer is done here by the titles of the individual pieces. In the Index below I have included proper names, mainly of writers, and also occurrences in the text of my own characteristic terms and themes—D.C.

Don Cupitt is a Life Fellow and former Dean of Emmanuel College, Cambridge, England, and the author of more than thirty books including, *Life, Life* (2003), *The Way to Happiness* (2005), and *The Great Questions of Life* (2006). A frequent broadcaster, mainly for the BBC, he has made three TV Series, one of which, "The Sea of Faith," (1984), gave rise to a book and to an international network of radical Christians which is still growing.